A New Owner's
Guide to
AFRICAN
GREY PARROTS

JG-705

T.F.H. Publications, Inc.
One TFH Plaza
Third and Union Avenues
Neptune City, NJ 07753

Library of Congress Cataloging-in-Publication Data
Moustaki, Nikki, 1970-
A new owner's guide to African grey parrots / Nikki Moustaki.
p. cm.
Includes index.
ISBN 0-7938-2855-4 (alk. paper)
1. African grey parrot. I. Title.
SF473.P3M67 2004
636.6'865—dc22
2004001447

www.tfh.com

A New Owner's
Guide to
African
Grey Parrots

Nikki Moustaki

Contents

2004 Edition

The Congo African Grey's most distinct trait is his ruby-red tail.

The Timneh African Grey Parrot has a dark-colored body and tail.

Toys are a necessity of the intelligent African Grey.

Make sure your Grey cannot fit his head between the bars of his cage.

It's best to feed your African Grey a variety of healthy foods.

African Greys are best known for their intelligence and personality.

INTRODUCING the African Grey Parrot

T he first thing people notice about the Grey is its beauty—the African Grey's feathers appear like a hand-scalloped costume of armor, like hundreds of perfect little seashells laid across each other to create a velvety gown for this intelligent and talkative bird. And let's not forget those ever-watchful eyes and that beautiful crimson tail. But it's this bird's personality and intelligence, beyond its good looks, that keeps people hooked.

The African Grey parrot has a history with humans dating back to biblical times, a fact that is no wonder to today's Grey owners—after all, these lucky people live with one of the most talented and beautiful birds alive, an animal able to charm royalty and researchers for centuries. Today, the African Grey is a favorite among expert bird keepers and novices alike.

SUBSPECIES AND ORIGINS

African Grey Parrots are recognized in two distinct subspecies: the Congo African Grey (*Psittacus erithacus erithacus*), also called the Red-tailed Grey; and the Timneh African Grey (*Psittacus erithacus timneh*). Because the African Grey's native range is so expansive, these birds tend to come in a variety of sizes and shades of gray, which can lead an owner to believe that he or she has a different "subspecies." However, the Congo and the Timneh are the only recognized subspecies of the African Grey Parrot.

Congo African Grey Parrot

The name "Congo African Grey" is actually a misnomer because the bird has a much wider natural

The Congo African Grey Parrot is recognizable by his bright scarlet-red tail, which reaches full coloring at maturity.

range than the Congo, but it is still the most common name for the red-tailed bird of this species, so you will see it throughout this book to represent that particular bird. The Congo Grey is found in the southeastern Ivory Coast, Kenya, and Tanzania.

Large Congos are sometimes called "Cameroons," because smugglers brought the birds into Cameroon and had that country written on the birds' export papers. Though a breeder may want to sell you a "Cameroon," know that it's simply a regular Congo that is, perhaps, a bit larger and lighter in color.

The Congo Grey is the more popularly kept of the two subspecies. The Congo is larger and its feathers are more prominently scalloped; it has a black beak and a bright-scarlet tail that reaches full coloring at maturity. (The tail is nearly black in a juvenile.)

Timneh African Grey Parrot

The Timneh is smaller than the Congo, with a darker-grey body and horn-colored beak, and its tail ranges in color from maroon to dark-gray or black. The Timneh is found in a smaller region along

the western edge of the Ivory Coast and through southern Guinea. The Congo tends to be more aloof, while the Timneh can be more of a family bird, though this varies from individual to individual. Both birds make equally good pets, and one should not be considered superior to the other.

GENERAL CHARACTERISTICS OF THE AFRICAN GREY

Every African Grey is an individual and has different personality quirks, just as humans do. Some African Greys will take readily to

The Timneh African Grey Parrot is slightly smaller than the Congo and has a darker-colored body, with a tail that is maroon, dark-gray, or even black.

strangers, while others will behave aggressively toward someone new or may suddenly become snappish toward a guardian for a period of time and begin to prefer someone else. Some will defend their cages, and others will bang the door repeatedly to get out—some even will learn how to open it. However, there are many general characteristics that are fairly consistent with all African Grey Parrots.

Personality

In general, most African Greys, when properly socialized, treated with kindness and respect, and given the proper housing, diet, and health care, make affectionate companions. Some African Greys go through a nipping phase or become aggressive and territorial, but most learn what is unacceptable behavior through an owner's actions and reactions.

If allowed to make choices, most well socialized African Greys would choose to play with their human companion for a good part of each day. However, many owners so tightly control the African Grey's daily life that the bird often becomes cranky and nippy. This is why it's a good idea to make sure you have the time to devote to this bird, so you're not simply playing with him for the hour between dinner and the evening news. African Greys can be taught to play on their own, but solitary play doesn't replace human interaction.

Wild African Grey babies learn to do things by watching their parents, so if you show your Grey how to have fun by himself, he'll learn. You can rip paper, break Popsicle sticks, and pretend to gnaw on wooden blocks in front of your Grey, and he'll soon get the idea. Greys pick up behaviors so quickly, you'll be surprised at how easily you can teach good behaviors—and unintentionally reinforce bad ones.

Sensitivity

The sensitivity of the African Grey is unrivaled among companion birds, with the possible exception of the cockatoo. This sensitivity is part of the Grey's charm, but it can also lead to common behavioral problems. Even a small change in daily routine or in the bird's surroundings can lead to plucking and crankiness—and an unhappy bird and unhappy human guardian.

Vocabulary and Vocalization

The myth of the loquacious Grey is more than just a myth. The

Grey is one of the top talkers among *psittacines* (parrots), and Grey fanciers will tell you that they are the best, able to repeat words and phrases that they have heard just a few times, perhaps even only once. Greys come into their full talking ability as they approach one year of age but may pick up a few words sooner than that. Not only will these birds develop outstanding vocabularies, but they may also come to understand what they are saying. However, even though these birds are known to talk up a storm, not all African Greys learn to talk. Some will learn a variety of other household sounds, as well as specific whistles.

Intelligence

Intelligence is probably one of the main factors that make the African Grey one of the most desirable companion birds available today. The African Grey is a highly intelligent individual, able to figure out how to escape from his cage and solve complicated puzzles. African Greys are said to have the intelligence equal to that of a four-year-old human child—that's a very smart bird! An African Grey will stun you with the things he is able to learn. For example,

Greys are highly intelligent birds that are able to solve complicated puzzles. Many can eventually understand the meaning of words and put them into context.

African Greys love spending time with their human companions, and most develop an intensely strong bond with them.

he may come to actually understand words and put them into context. This means that he is not simply mimicking but actually talking. Never underestimate this highly intelligent creature.

Your Grey may learn to understand things if you take the time to teach him. For example, explain to your bird everything you are doing. If you are offering carrots, say, "Carrots" as you present them to him. If you are going into another room, tell your Grey that's what you're doing. Your bird will come to understand what these things actually mean and may begin really communicating with you. If you say, "Do you want a head scratch?" every time you scratch your bird's head, he may say the phrase back to you when he desires a head rub. My Grey fully comprehends the meaning of "Come here," and he constantly calls me over to his play gym.

The most famous Grey of all, Alex, and his owner, Dr. Irene Pepperberg, made the intelligence of this species well known. Alex, a Congo African Grey, is the continuing subject of a research study conducted by Dr. Pepperberg and her students at the University of Arizona. Using specialized techniques that involve repetition and reward, the researchers have taught Alex and three other Grey parrots to count, identify objects, shapes, colors, and materials, and to know the concepts of "same" and "different." The birds also boss around lab assistants in order to modify their environment.

There is even evidence to suggest that Alex may be able to read some day. This shows that Greys are capable of far more than just mimicry. Furthermore, Alex is actually able to think in terms of abstract concepts, and he is able to quantify objects with over an 80-percent accuracy rate. This means that when you take an African Grey into your home as a pet, you are living with a creature that is able to understand what you are saying to the degree of a four-year-old child. That's a lot of animal! However, because this species is so intelligent, boredom and inactivity can often lead to frustration.

Beyond the medical and emotional issues stemming from boredom and stress due to this bird's intelligent nature, there's the issue of living with another species that may often outwit you. This is a bird that can easily manipulate his owner into giving him more attention. However, many guardians feel blessed to live with an animal that can communicate its needs so clearly.

Because researchers have had such great success with Alex, Dr. Pepperberg is training another one of her Greys to use the Internet. Pepperberg hopes that parrots will eventually have access to the World Wide Web and will surf websites to alleviate their boredom; perhaps they will even be able to videoconference with their friends.

Social Interaction and Companionship

Greys are highly social animals that appreciate each other's company in the wild or their human's company in captivity. Your Grey will want to be with you 24 hours a day. Be sure you have the time to spend with this sensitive bird before you purchase one. A lonely Grey will languish and may begin plucking, excessive vocalization, and biting in reaction to this loneliness.

Most well socialized African Greys will do *anything* to be close to the one they love. The human/African Grey bond can be a strong one, lasting the bird's lifetime. African Greys make especially good companions when they are acquired as hand-fed youngsters.

The way you behave around your African Grey and the way you interact with him has everything to do with what kind of a pet he will make. If you play roughly with your bird, expect the bird to play roughly back. However, if you treat the bird gently and calmly, you will find that he will respond favorably to your actions. Speak softly, handle the bird gently, and respect his needs. For example, if your bird doesn't want to come out of his cage at the precise moment that you want him to come out, you may have to wait a few minutes and try again. It's important to allow your bird to make some choices concerning his daily life—after all, in the wild, these birds do not have human companions dictating their every move.

If you want your African Grey to be very tame and sweet, you will have to play with him frequently and socialize him properly into the household. African Greys that get a lot of hands-on attention become fiercely bonded to their humans and will remain loyal companions. An African Grey left alone for too long may begin to lose his affectionate quality and may become neurotic, self-mutilating, or nippy—and it's not fun to be nipped or bitten by that formidable beak. This is why the African Grey is a good companion only when his human plans to allot a generous amount of time to spend with him. A bird is not a good companion for someone who wants a "sometimes" pet.

Some species of birds will react with the same gusto and friendliness to every member of the family—but not so with Greys. The Timneh may be more capable of accepting family members than the Congo, but as with all birds, behavior is highly individual. Nevertheless, Greys can be socialized to accept every member of the family. Your

If you expose your Grey to many people and things while he is young, he will be more socialized and accepting of new things throughout his life.

bird's behavior depends largely on how you treat him and socialize him from the beginning.

Though African Greys come with certain inherent behaviors and requirements, how you socialize your bird is the most important factor determining how you and your bird get along and how happy your bird will be in the long term. If you expose your Grey to many people and things while he is young, he will have more tolerance for new things later in life. For example, I got my first Grey in the spring, and when winter rolled around and I brought out my winter hats, my Grey freaked out the first time I put one on. I had to take off the hat, show him what it was, put it on in front of him, and let him know that the hat was harmless. We haven't had that problem since.

Affection

The African Grey shows his affection for his human companion by performing a number of seemingly strange behaviors. Many will try to kiss their humans on the mouth. (This is not recommended, as the human mouth contains bacteria that aren't good for an African Grey, though a kiss on the head or the top of the beak is fine.) An African Grey will often regurgitate to its human as a sign of ultimate affection—the notion of vomiting as affection is ghastly, but it's actually a very charming gesture that means the Grey has

African Greys are social birds, and some may even enjoy snuggling or petting.

chosen you as his beloved. Most Greys love to be scratched on the neck, and yours may put his head down, offering his neck for a good scratching. This is a very vulnerable position for the Grey and it is a sign that the bird trusts you.

Even though Greys are social birds, they are not often the cuddliest. Often, people will buy birds and expect to be able to hug and caress their new feathered friends. Greys will enjoy head scratching and perhaps a caress or two, but they do not appreciate intense physical contact, though some don't mind some

Because of its superior intelligence, the Grey has complex emotional and psychological needs and will require a lot of attention.

snuggling and petting. Every bird is an individual and will have individual tastes and preferences. Some Greys want nothing more than to sit in their owners' laps, snuggled in a towel or blanket, having their little heads caressed, while others will be far more aloof.

Is the African Grey For You?

The African Grey makes a great companion, is long-lived and loyal, and can become extremely attached to humans. You will not "have" an African Grey—an African Grey will "have" you. This bird is one of the most sensitive and intelligent of the parrots available as companions today, but these traits sometimes make the species difficult to care for, too. Only the most devoted bird keeper will be able to properly care for this bird. The following section outlines some important things you should consider before making the final decision to bring an African Grey into your home.

An African Grey's Special Needs

The African Grey needs far more than food and water to survive—he has complex emotional and psychological needs that an owner must understand and provide for. If these needs are not met, Greys can become depressed, bored, and neurotic, feelings that can lead to self-mutilating behaviors. There is much debate as to whether or not animals have feelings, but anyone that lives with an African Grey will answer a resounding, "*Yes!*" to this question.

An African Grey's needs are many but they are easy to provide for, though this is sometimes time-consuming. An African Grey needs proper housing and nutrition, time out of the cage, a safe place to play and things to play with, veterinarian visits (even when well), and an observant, attentive, devoted companion—you. This is a bird that needs constant attention and guidance, one that enjoys learning and interaction with his "flock." When you buy an African Grey, truly evaluate whether or not you have the time and patience to deal with this sensitive bird.

Noise Level

African Greys are not known to be loud, insistently noisy parrots, but they can certainly learn to screech if taught to do so. If your household is particularly noisy, with lots of loud talking and activity, expect that your Grey will pick this up. If you have another bird, a noisy Amazon parrot, for example, your Grey will pick up his raucous call. Greys are also notorious for picking up mechanical noises, particularly car alarms, alarm clocks, and the beeping of a microwave or answering machine. These are all machines that make the Grey's humans jump up and rush around. The Grey soon comes to associate these noises with an action on his human's part and will mimic the noise to create the same effect.

If you reinforce the noise by picking the bird up or reacting verbally to the insistent mimicking of your alarm clock, your Grey will keep making the noise. If you ignore the noise, your Grey will realize that it has no effect and may pick up another, more acceptable noise or phrase when he wants attention. I've been able to replace annoying noises by singing the musical "warm-up scale" (la la la . . .) and reinforcing the singing with praise and attention when I hear him doing it. We sing together often.

Mess

Like most parrots, African Greys are messy. Food will find its way onto the floor and walls. Greys also like to shred paper and will do so with gusto. They aren't really fond of eliminating in their cages, so they will often make sure their wastes land on the floor. If you are infuriated by mess or are a die-hard neatnik, an African Grey (or any bird) may not be the pet for you. There are cage accessories and acrylic cages that help to prevent mess, but there's not much that will eliminate it.

Expenses

The African Grey is a pricey bird to begin with, but it's the cage and the accessories that really put a dent in your wallet. Once you make the initial purchases, however, upkeep of an African Grey is fairly inexpensive, though cost is relative, depending on how creative you can be with homemade toys. Keep in mind that African Greys can be highly destructive, and if you don't take precautions, a single African Grey can seriously damage antiques or other expensive items, not to mention injure himself, on items he should not have contact with. This is why it's important to "African Grey-proof" your home before your begin living with your new pet.

Time Concerns

An African Grey needs a good deal of attention to maintain the proper level of physical and mental health. An African Grey that is ignored or neglected will become unhappy and neurotic, and he may begin to mutilate himself by picking out or chewing his feathers or other parts of his body. Even African Greys that

Living with your African Grey will come with many responsibilities, but the companionship you will receive will make it all worthwhile.

live in pairs need human attention. An observant owner who takes the time to notice the behavioral patterns of his or her birds is an owner that can prevent illness and save lives.

It also takes a good bit of time to provide the daily and weekly care that an African Grey needs to remain healthy. Cage and accessory cleaning might add up to four hours or more a week. Cleaning the mess that an African Grey makes takes time as well. There might be times when you will have to cancel a social outing or take half a day off of work to take your African Grey to the veterinarian in the case of an illness or accident. A person with a heavy work schedule or someone who travels frequently may not have the time required to properly take care of this animal.

Responsibilities

As with any companion animal, a certain set of responsibilities comes with living with an African Grey. Welcome these tasks! An African Grey provides his human with as many as 50 years of companionship, and a person should be willing to provide his or her pet bird with what he needs to live out his life in comfort, health, and happiness.

The following is a list of the many responsibilities that come with African Grey ownership.

- Daily cleaning of the cage.
- A weekly, more thorough cleaning of the cage and surrounding area.
- Providing fresh water at least twice a day.
- Presenting a healthy diet, including fresh fruits, vegetables, and safe table foods daily.
- Offering safe playtime out of the cage daily.
- Watching closely for signs of illness and taking your African Grey to the veterinarian if you suspect something is wrong or in the event of an accident.
- African Grey-proofing your home so that it's a safe place for him to play.
- Watching other pets closely when your African Grey is out of his cage.
- Checking the cage and toys daily for dangerous wear-and tear.
- Ensuring that your African Grey is neither too warm nor too cold and is housed in a spot that is free of drafts.

Think of your relationship with your Grey as a friendship, not simply an owner/ pet relationship.

IS EXPERIENCE NECESSARY?

Buying a bird with this amount of intelligence and sensitivity takes a lot of thought and possibly some knowledge of how to care properly for birds in general. You may want to wait until you've got some experience under your "birdy belt" before you undertake the responsibility of this sensitive bird with a lifespan of more than 50 years. Most inexperienced bird owners may find themselves between a rock and a hard place with this advice. Someone may really want a Grey but find himself or herself talked out of the purchase by a breeder or pet shop owner, who may direct that individual to a smaller, more easily cared for bird instead. If you're willing to do a lot of research and create a relationship with a breeder, an avian expert, and other people experienced with Greys, then you may be able to handle this species as a first bird.

Make sure that the person from whom you purchase the bird is willing to work with you to make you and the bird as happy as possible. Because Greys are so sensitive, you should take a look at your own lifestyle and ask yourself whether this bird will be a good addition to your family or whether you will both be unhappy living together. If you do decide to get a Grey or you already have one, think of your relationship more as a friendship rather than owner/ pet. If you respect your bird as you would a good friend, you'll be at an advantage with the Grey, which won't take well to being treated like a "mere bird."

AFRICAN GREYS AND CHILDREN

Because the African Grey uses his beak to explore his world, and because that beak is strong and hard, the African Grey might not be the best pet for a child. A Timneh Grey may be a good pet for an older child, perhaps one who is older than ten years of age. It is necessary that the child understands that the African Grey is an individual with likes and dislikes of his own, and he may not always want to play when the child is ready. The Timneh is a little hardier and more able to accept changes in his environment than a Congo.

Children tend to have short attention spans, and some children may become disinterested with the African Grey over time. This is a sad state for the African Grey, because he will bond closely with the child and will not take well to being ignored. Also remember that a child will grow up during the African Grey's lifetime and may move

If you have other pet birds in your home, judge the personality of those birds carefully before making the decision to add an African Grey to the family.

on to bigger things, like college or marriage, and may not be able to take the bird along. A child who receives an African Grey at 10 years of age might have that same bird until the "child" is 60 years old!

African Greys and Other Pets

African Greys have a tendency not to get along with other pets, and this is a huge consideration for people who have other animals in the home. African Greys can pose a danger to other birds in the home if they are allowed to mingle. There are exceptions to this rule, however, so you will have to judge the characters of your particular birds.

African Greys can fall prey to just about any other pet you may own. A dog or cat, for example, can be dangerous for an African Grey, because they will see him as prey or a toy. One little scratch during "play" is enough to kill an African Grey. Ferrets and pet rats may also hunt your African Grey, and a fish tank or bowl poses a drowning threat if your Grey is allowed to roam free in your home without supervision.

If you have other birds, make sure that they get along well, or if you have dogs, cats, or other small animals, make sure that they do not have the chance to "get together." *Never* think that it's "cute" to introduce your African Grey to a predator—this is just asking for trouble. This breed of bird is highly susceptible to trauma, and one negative incident can change the bird's behavior patterns for life.

Commitment

Many people think that just because African Greys are birds and have "bird brains," they cannot get lonely or anxious. This assumption couldn't be more wrong. A lonely or mistreated African Grey can develop illnesses and self-mutilating behaviors, which can be deadly. If you do take on an African Grey as a companion, think ahead to what you're going to be doing for the rest of your life. Are there going to be any major life changes? Will you be able to care for this bird for the long term? An African Grey can live 40 to 50 years or more with the proper care. What will you be doing 50 years from now? Make a solid commitment to your bird to care for him for the duration of his life, and make arrangements for your bird should he outlive you.

CHOOSING the Perfect African Grey

Choosing the perfect African Grey might seem as easy as visiting your local pet shop and picking out the most attractive one. That's certainly one way of doing it, but it's not the most informed way to choose a companion that could potentially be a member of your family for more than 40 to 50 years—a companion you may have to will to your children or grandchildren. If you've already bought an African Grey on impulse, don't fret—this chapter will help should you want another one.

MAKING THE RIGHT CHOICES

There are several important decisions that go into choosing the right African Grey for your family. Begin by making a list of all of the factors that you wish for in a pet bird. Do you want to train your African Grey to be friendly, or do you want one that will play with you the first day you bring him home? Do you want a Timneh African Grey or a Congo? How much do you want to spend? Do you want one that's already talking or a newly weaned baby that you will have to teach to talk? The following are some factors you will want to consider.

Species

The Congo African Grey, easily distinguishable by its bright-red tail, is known to be highly sensitive. The smaller, darker Timneh African Grey, on the other hand, is a little hardier and more accepting of change. Both birds are excellent talkers. The Congo is pricier than the Timneh, but that doesn't mean the Timneh is an inferior companion. On the contrary, the Timneh makes an excellent companion and is more likely to accept several people as friends than the Congo will, making it a great family bird.

Remember, however, that each bird has his own individual personality; it's more important to choose an individual bird that you like than to choose a particular species. When you choose a bird, make sure he has all of the qualities that you want. Each Grey is a little bit different, just as each dog, cat, horse, or human is a little bit different.

Hand-Raised or Parent-Raised?

A hand-raised African Grey, that is, one that has been taken out of the nest when he was young and handfed by a human caregiver, makes a far better hands-on companion than a parent-raised African Grey does. African Greys are extremely spirited and self-directed—they do what they want to do when they want to do it. A hand-raised African Grey will actually *want* to play with you all the time. An African Grey that was raised by his parents will not see a human owner as a playmate until he is trained to do so, and he may shy from contact initially. However, African Greys are not difficult birds to train once you develop mutual trust.

Just like humans, each African Grey is an individual, so choose an individual whose personality fits your own.

Most responsible pet shops and breeders will not sell you a baby African Grey that is still eating baby bird formula. It is not a good idea for you to try to feed your baby African Grey by hand—if you are inexperienced with hand-feeding, you may seriously you're your baby bird. It's better to leave the hand-feeding to someone who knows how to do it. Your African Grey will not be any less bonded to you when fed by someone else. You're the one who will care for him on a daily basis, and he will come to see you as a friend if you handle him regularly with gentleness and affection. Hand-feeding socializes a baby African Grey to enjoy contact with humans. Often, the hand-feeder will take the time to play with and hold the babies, making them very tame and sweet.

You can tell that an African Grey has been hand-fed by handling him. If he doesn't bite and is tame and calm, it is likely that someone socialized him to enjoy human contact. An African Grey that hides in the corner of his cage, attacks, or growls might not make the best pet right away—you will have to take substantial time to tame and socialize this bird.

Age

If you want a very affectionate companion, it's best to buy an African Grey just after it has been weaned off of baby formula and is eating on its own. Each species has a different weaning time. African Grey babies should be ready for a new home at about 16 weeks of age, though some breeders keep them longer to make sure the babies are eating well on their own. An older African Grey can make a wonderful pet as well if he has been handled regularly, is tame, and has a sweet temperament.

Greys that were not handled regularly at a young age often "revert" as they grow older and lose the ability to be handled easily, becoming skittish, nippy, destructive, or just plain vicious. These birds do need a loving home, but only consider taking on a neglected bird if you have the time and patience to work with him.

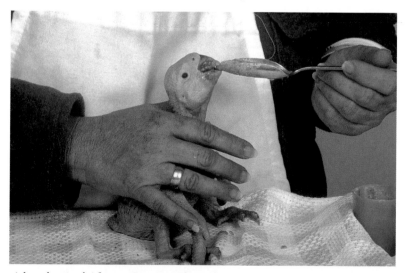

A hand-raised African Grey, one that is hand-fed by a human caregiver from a very young age, will be easily socialized and will want to play with you all of the time.

Because Greys are monomorphic, you may not be able to determine whether your bird is a male or female. However, both sexes make equally good companion birds.

Remember, an African Grey can live a very long time, so a two or three-year-old African Grey is still essentially a youngster. Don't pass by the African Grey that is a little older—he can make just as good a companion as a very young baby if he has been properly socialized. You can tell a juvenile Congo African Grey by his dark eyes and the dark tips at the end of its red tail feathers. The juvenile Timneh will have a very dark tail that gets lighter as the bird matures. As both birds mature, they will develop yellow eyes, though the pupils will remain black.

Male or Female?

African Greys are monomorphic, meaning that there are no distinguishable characteristics between the males and the females of the species. You will not be able to determine the sex of the bird you are buying. However, sex should not be a consideration when you are buying a pet African Grey—both sexes make equally good companion animals. You can choose a gender-neutral name for your pet in case you find out his or her sex later.

Females often lay eggs when they become sexually mature, a sure sign that you have a hen. If you want to know the sex of your bird, you can have a simple and painless DNA test done, either through

African Greys that are bonded to other birds can still develop a bond with their human companions.

a blood sample taken by your veterinarian or by sending a feather to a laboratory that conducts such tests. The DNA test is 100 percent effective in determining sex.

How Many?

A single African Grey can make a better hands-on pet than African Greys kept in a pair, though this is not always the case—African Greys that are bonded to another bird can have a bird "friend" and still love their person-friend. In the case of a single African Grey, you act as his "mate," providing the love and affection he needs to be happy. Keeping one African Grey alone in a cage with no human or bird contact is cruel.

If your pet is not getting the attention you once provided due to a lifestyle change, consider getting him a friend. However, your established bird may become very jealous of the "interloper" and refuse to accept him. If this becomes the case, you will then have *two* Greys to please. If you do bring another bird (or other pet or human infant) into the home, be sure to interact with the already established Grey before you play with the newcomer.

WHERE TO ACQUIRE YOUR AFRICAN GREY

For many people, the African Grey is an impulse buy from a pet shop, a purchase made with the heart. Often, buyer's remorse sets in once the owner learns of all the details involved with caring for a bird, especially if he becomes persistently noisy, becomes aggressive and bites, or becomes ill. Buying the right African Grey, one that's healthy and properly socialized to humans, is easy once you've found a shop or a breeder that cares for their young birds correctly.

General Pet Shops

Most pet shops carry a variety of birds along with their other animals. Therefore, it is important to choose one that has employees who know about the birds sold there. Ask the staff a lot of questions and see if there is a health guarantee available. If you sense that the employees are knowledgeable, the birds seem well cared for, the cages are clean, and all of the birds have fresh food and water, then you can feel comfortable choosing your perfect African Grey at this establishment.

Bird Specialty Shops

A shop that sells only birds and bird supplies is another option for finding your African Grey. The staff in a bird shop deals only with birds and troubleshoots bird problems with customers all day long. They are trained to know how an ill bird behaves and may know something about the history and personality of your particular bird. Often, bird shops are willing to provide a new owner with a health guarantee and require a visit to the veterinarian to make the guarantee complete. Always ask for a health guarantee before buying a bird, and get it in writing before you leave the store.

Make sure the African Grey you obtain is healthy and well cared for.

African Grey Parrot Breeders

An African Grey breeder is another resource for obtaining an African Grey Parrot. African Grey breeders are dedicated to the species and knowledgeable about the care and training of these birds. An African Grey breeder is likely to help mentor you through the trials of African Grey ownership. This is someone who cares about the lives of his or her baby African Greys and will be available to answer any questions you might have about raising your new feathered friend.

Rescue Organizations

Many animal shelters and bird rescue organizations regularly have African Greys up for adoption. Because this is a strong-willed, destructive bird that is prone to feather plucking, many African Greys find themselves out of a home. You may want to put yourself on a list at your local shelter in case they get an African Grey in for adoption. Remember that this bird might come with some quirks and will need extra patience and love in order for him to thrive in his new home. Change is difficult on a bird, so be aware that a rescued African Grey might be anxious until he becomes adjusted to his new home.

A bird rescue organization in particular is a great place to go if you want to give a home to an African Grey that has been given up for adoption. Sadly, many companion birds typically only live in a home for two to three years before they are shuffled along to the next place, and as a result, there are plenty of homeless birds needing a family to call their own. Do an Internet search on "rescue birds" or call your local shelter to have your name put on an adoption list.

BUY FROM A REPUTABLE SOURCE

It is absolutely important to buy from a reputable source because the African Grey Parrot is one of the many species of animals on a list as part of the Convention of International Trade in Endangered Species (CITES) treaty, and as such is banned from commercial international trade. If you have a young African Grey, it was probably domestically bred, which is far better for the environment, for your bird, and for his parents than if he was trapped in the wild. The CITES treaty was drawn to protect wildlife from overexploitation and from the risk of the threat of extinction. If, for some reason, you suspect that a bird you are going to purchase is smuggled, do not go through with the purchase. Instead, buy from a reputable breeder or bird shop.

How to Choose a Healthy African Grey

A healthy African Grey is busy and energetic, bright and attentive, and presents a good attitude. A healthy African Grey has bright eyes, clear nares (nostrils), a clean vent, and is free of debris on his feathers, which should be tight and shiny and cover the entire bird with no patches of skin showing (with the exception of around the face where there is a whitish patch of bare skin). His feet are clean and intact, and he eats with gusto. He clambers around the cage, plays with his toys, and seems lively in general. When he sleeps, he does so on a perch, usually sitting on one leg. It is important to choose an African Grey that has these qualities.

An African Grey that is not feeling well may be fluffed up and sitting on the cage floor in a corner, looking depressed. He may have discharge from his eyes or nares and a messy vent. His feathers

A healthy African Grey should have bright eyes, shiny feathers, clean feet, and he should be energetic and attentive.

might be dirty from lack of grooming, and he may even have patches of feathers missing. He may look sleepy and droopy, puffing his feathers to retain body heat. This is not an African Grey you want to take home, even out of pity.

THE FIRST FEW DAYS AT HOME

When you first bring your African Grey home, you will want to give him a few pressure-free days to adjust to the new environment. This is not the time to begin heavy training sessions or long play sessions away from the cage. Change is difficult on an African Grey, a creature that thrives on routine.

Think of your African Grey's life before you decided to take him home—he was bred and hand-fed in one place, sold to another

If you see an African Grey eating heartily, it's usually a sign of good health.

It is a good idea to offer your Grey treats when you first bring him home. Eating in his new home will help your Grey adjust, and treats will be a tempting offer.

place, and is now moving to a third location—that's a lot of adjustment for a bird! Also, if the bird is young, he may be "clumsy" in his new location. Greys are notorious for their clumsiness, but "clumsy" is not really the right word—it's more like they're not perfectly suited for life in a human home. Greys in the wild are certainly not "clumsy;" they are graceful and comfortable in their environment. However, Greys in a home are presented with a lot of unusual obstacles, and young Greys often need to adjust to all the accoutrements that come with living in a human environment.

The first thing you should do is set up your new friend's cage and put it in his permanent place. This way you won't be adding toys and cups while your African Grey is simply trying to relax. Once you've placed your African Grey in his new cage and given him fresh food and water, leave him alone in quiet for a few hours so that he can get adjust to his new situation and scenery.

Offer treats at this time. It's a good sign of adjustment when your African Grey begins to eat and make noise. If he's cowering and hiding behind toys, trying to be invisible, he may need more time

You and your bird will become fast friends if you play with him every day for the first few weeks. Your Grey will also develop a delightful personality with this attention.

to adjust. Be patient—he will come around eventually. Don't think that your new bird is boring because he's scared—you would be scared, too. Speak softly to him and introduce yourself and other family members.

After a day or so you can begin bringing your African Grey out of his cage for playtime. If the bird is a baby, gently scoop him off of the perch or side of the cage, making sure not to pull hard on his feet, which may be clutching whatever he's standing on. A baby doesn't yet know to step onto your hand—you will have to teach him to do this by asking him to "step up" each time you present your hand. Don't expect too much from your African Grey at first—you're both getting used to each other.

Each African Grey has a different personality and different favorite things. You will learn all about your new bird as the days go on. In this initial stage, move calmly around the bird and play with him very gently. This is the time to build your relationship together, the time when your bird will learn to trust you and see you as a friend. If you force an interaction at this fragile time, you may only succeed in scaring your bird, and he will remember you as someone to be feared, not trusted.

If you play with your bird every day for the first few weeks, perhaps even fielding a few uncomfortable nips with composure, you'll find that your African Grey will develop a sparkling, lively personality and that the two of you will become fast friends. The change from baby bird to adolescent happens rapidly, and once he begins to mature, an African Grey will show you how fun a friend he can be.

QUARANTINE

If you have other birds, you should definitely quarantine your African Grey when you first bring him home. Quarantine is traditionally a period of 40 days in which a new bird is kept separate from birds already established in the household. Some people choose to shorten this period to 30 days and find no harm in doing so.

During the period of quarantine, a new bird is watched for signs of illness. You should feed and water the new bird after you care for your other birds and change your clothing and disinfect your hands after any contact with the bird or its cage. Quarantine is the only way to prevent a new bird from passing a potential illness to the birds you already own. It is sometimes not possible to completely separate a new bird from established birds, but you should try to do your best to keep contact at a minimum while the new bird is being quarantined.

HOUSING Your African Grey

O nce you've decided on the species of African Grey you're going to add to your family and have chosen your particular bird, you need to consider proper housing. Choosing the right cage can mean the difference between having a safe, happy African Grey and having one that's bound for injury—or worse. There are many housing options available at your local pet shop, but not all of them are acceptable choices. Providing your African Grey with the right kind of housing and accessories is a major way to ensure his well-being and comfort.

Many people don't like the idea of keeping a bird in a cage—birds are supposed to be free, right? Yes, that's true, but the home offers many dangers for your curious African Grey. Supervised out-of-cage time is a necessary part of your African Grey's life, but an unsupervised African Grey might get in harm's way—and fast! You might also be surprised at the damage an African Grey's beak can do to items in a home. A cage will keep your bird safe and out of mischief when you're away.

An African Grey housed in the proper kind of cage with the appropriate accessories often loves his cage and thinks of it as his home, a comfortable place to eat, play, and sleep. A cage is not meant to be a prison, but a safe space for your bird to reside while you're unable to supervise him or when he wants a timeout from the hectic life of his "flock."

FINDING THE RIGHT CAGE

The right kind of cage isn't hard to find if you know what you're looking for. Most pet shops should carry appropriate housing for your Grey, but you may have pick through the selection to find what you want. Don't let the pet store staff push you into buying something you feel is inappropriate for your pet. If you don't see a cage that you like, there are plenty of catalogs or online retailers that should carry what you need.

Proper Size

Wild African Greys spend most of their days winging around, foraging for food, searching for water, and, at certain times of year, nesting—that's a lot of activity. A companion African Grey lives a far different life, but his energy level can surely compete with that of his wild cousins. Your companion African Grey is a bird that doesn't like to just sit around. A healthy, well-socialized Grey should spend plenty of time moving, climbing, chewing things to bits, and flapping his wings. African Greys are animals on the go.

Because of their high energy level, African Greys need a rather large space in which to spend their days. Unfortunately, most store-bought cages are too small and don't allow the African Grey to expend his energy, which can be turned upon

When choosing a cage, always remember that bigger is better. Make sure your Grey will have plenty of room to stretch his wings and to fly from perch to perch.

himself in the form of self-mutilation. Most pet store personnel don't know much about birds, unless you're shopping in a really good all-bird store. The person helping you may suggest too small a cage. Remember, when it comes to birdcages, bigger is better.

An African Grey forced to spend his days housed in a very confined space will be extremely unhappy. Birds are creatures of boundless space, and even though your African Grey was raised in captivity, his instincts tell him that being confined is unnatural. If your African Grey is going to spend a good portion of the day housed in a cage, be sure to buy the largest that your space and budget can afford. Ideally, your bird should be able to actually fly from perch to perch—this means that it should take wing power to get from one side of the cage to the other.

Most cages only allow the bird to clamber on the bars to move around, but these cages are too small, unless the bird has a large play gym and is allowed a lot of out-of-cage time. The exception to this rule is the very young Grey, which will appreciate a smaller cage for the first few months at home. A baby Grey is not yet as nimble as an older Grey and can develop a fear of falling, which will be exaggerated in a large cage. If you want to purchase only one cage, you can remedy this fear by placing perches and ladders at the bottom of the large cage and raising them as the baby becomes more skilled at climbing.

Proper Shape

The perfect shape for an African Grey cage is a large square or a large, long rectangle. Corners in a cage will make an African Grey feel comfortable. A round cage might be attractive but offers far less security than a square cage, unless the round cage is extremely large.

The bars on the African Grey's cage should be primarily horizontal, with a few vertical bars for structural purposes. Horizontal bars allow the African Grey to climb around his cage and hang safely on the side.

The proper shape for an African Grey's cage should be a large square or a large, long rectangle.

Proper Materials

The proper material for an African Grey cage is stainless steel, powder-coated steel, or wrought iron. Other metals may contain harmful toxins, and coating on the cage bars is a tempting "treat" for the African Grey, which may ingest these harmful materials and become ill or die. Acrylic cages are a nice choice for the African Grey because the solid walls prevent mess, though they don't allow for climbing, are often too small, and can be quite pricey. Caging materials bought from the hardware store for a homemade cage are often dipped in zinc, which is deadly for birds. Before you build a cage, scrub the wire well with a stiff brush and let it "cure" out in the rain and sun for a few weeks, until the outer coating has worn off.

A Grey's cage should be made out of stainless steel, powder-coated steel, or wrought iron.

Safe Doors

Commercially made cages commonly come with three types of doors. The best types of doors for the African Grey are the doors that open downward (like an oven door) or to the side (like your front door). Doors that slide up and down (like a guillotine) are the most common type for a smaller cage but can cause your bird serious injury. African Greys are extremely good escape artists and can quickly learn how to open the doors to their cages—consider buying spring clips or another type of lock so that your bird can't escape, or buy cages that have self-locking doors (though a savvy Grey may learn to manipulate these, too.)

The Cage Bottom

The proper cage for an African Grey is one that has a grating or a grill on the bottom that prevents the bird from rolling around in his own mess. African Greys are notorious for digging, shredding paper, and tossing things in their water, and there's nothing an African Grey would like more than to be able to get to the material on the cage bottom and play there. This is exceptionally unsanitary and can lead to serious illness.

In the wild, African Greys are never exposed to their own fecal materials the way they are in a caged environment. You should take

Cage bars should be spaced so that your Grey can't fit his head through the gaps. The bars on this cage are appropriately spaced.

care that your bird is exposed to as little of his own waste material as possible—a grate on the bottom of the cage will help facilitate this. Many Greys refuse to defecate in the cage and will hang over the side to eliminate on the floor. In this case, you will simply have to place a piece of newspaper or other material in that spot.

Improper Housing: Buyer Beware

Tall cages shaped like pagodas or other fancy structures are too tall and narrow for the African Grey because he likes a lot of horizontal space to clamber around in. Cages with more vertical space than horizontal space are wasted on the African Grey.

Ornate, showy cages are inappropriate as well. Elaborate scrollwork on a cage can catch your African Grey's toes or leg band, causing serious injury. Cages with bars that are thickly painted or covered with plastic or other materials are terrible choices for the African Grey; he will spend most of the day picking the material off the bars. These materials can be toxic, or at least harmful and can cause death if ingested. Powder-coated cages are acceptable, however. You can find these in most stores or catalogs.

Cage bars should be spaced so that your African Grey can't poke his head through them—he might not be able to get his head out again, like a child with his or her head stuck in a banister. Having his head stuck can cause your African Grey to panic, which can lead to a broken neck or strangulation.

Remember—just because a cage is for sale in the pet shop, doesn't mean that it's safe or proper housing for your pet.

PLACING THE CAGE

Now that you've decided on a cage, you have to consider where in your home your African Grey is going to live. This is an important decision that can make the difference between a very happy bird and a miserable one.

Choosing the Room

Try to look at this from your African Grey's perspective—it might be convenient for you to house your bird in the garage, but is he going to receive enough attention, light, fresh air, and warmth there? Probably not. Your African Grey's cage is best placed in a location that gets a lot of traffic, like the family room or living room. A place where there's too much swift-moving traffic, like a hallway, isn't a great location, however. The cage should be in an area where there's a sense of relative calm but that is well attended by family members

Because your African Grey needs a good deal of attention, an out-of-the-way location isn't the best choice—he will begin to miss his "flock" (you and your family) immediately if relegated to a back room. The garage is too drafty and is prone to fumes. The bathroom and kitchen are both places that are prone to wide temperature ranges and chemicals, neither of which are healthy for an African

When selecting a room for cage placement, choose one that gets a lot of traffic, like the family room or living room.

Grey. A child's room might be dark and quiet for most of the day while the child is at school and too noisy at other times. Again, the family room or living room is your best bet.

Choosing a Corner

Once you've decided on the room where your African Grey is going to live, choose a corner location for the cage, which will make your bird feel safe. A cage that's standing or hanging in the middle of the room will make for an insecure bird. When the family cat appears or a car backfires outside, your African Grey may want to retreat to the back of the cage—a cage that's freestanding will have no "back," no place for the bird to "hide."

To make your African Grey feel even more secure, especially if you can't place the cage next to a wall, you can surround it with safe, nontoxic plants. Be aware that an African Grey will make quick work of a plant, chewing it to bits, so you should carefully supervise him when he's out of the cage.

The corner where the cage is set up should be free of drafts. Don't place the cage directly in front of a window, even though this seems like the thing to do. Your African Grey really doesn't need a great view. African Greys are extremely alert creatures and will become alarmed by predators lurking outside—these predators can take the form of the neighbor's cat or dog, hawks circling in the sky, rats, raccoons, and even cars going by. Imagine having to be on guard all the time. Also, the sun shining in a window may overheat your bird if he can't get out of the sunlight. It's okay for your African Grey to be placed near a window but not directly in front of it, unless the cage is so large that part of it extends over onto a wall.

Outdoor Risks

Placing a commercial cage outside on a patio or porch is extremely risky. For one, your African Grey will be very vulnerable to predators outside, and a cage is no match for a determined raccoon or opossum. A thief might be tempted to steal your African Grey, cage and all. Furthermore, the companion African Grey housed on a patio might not get as much attention as he would if he were housed in a family room. Some people choose to house multiple African Greys in large cages on an enclosed patio or porch—in this case, the African Greys have each other for company, and the cage is far too large for a thief to steal.

A cage on a patio should be double-wired, meaning it should have two layers of wire placed one over the other such that a predator would not be able to get to the feet of the birds inside—a rat or raccoon can actually pull parts of a bird through the wires of a cage. Also, if you live in a place that gets very hot or very cold, you might want to seriously consider housing your African Grey inside. Remember, this is a sensitive, intelligent bird that is prone to biting and plucking if neglected.

CAGE ACCESSORIES

Now that you've gotten the proper cage and found the perfect location in your home for your African Grey to live, you've got to furnish the cage with all of the necessities and goodies that your pet will need to be happy and healthy. You might be surprised at how many items you will have to buy, but many of these are one-time purchases and should last the lifetime of your bird.

Perches

Most commercial cages come with a couple of smooth, wooden dowels to use as perches. These are fine to use, but these perches

In order to prevent foot disorders or boredom, offer your Grey a variety of perches made of different sizes and materials.

Wooden perches are the standard choice and are also great for chewing.

alone do not serve as an adequate selection for an African Grey, which spends most of his life on his feet.

An African Grey that stands on the same perch day after day may develop foot sores and lameness, among other foot disorders. These are easily remedied by offering various perches made of assorted materials in many different dimensions. Your African Grey should have perches that make him stand with his feet very spread out (almost flat) and perches that allow his toes to almost touch each other when he's gripping them. The best dimension for a perch is one that allows the foot to form a half-circle. Fortunately, there are many different types of perches on the market, and they are easily found at your local pet store.

Wooden

Perches made of wood are the standard choice. However, the smooth, wooden dowels that come with a commercial cage don't offer much "footing" for your African Grey. You can remedy this by scoring the dowels every half-inch or so with a razor blade—this will give them more texture, and they will be easier to grip. Manzanita wood and cholla wood perches are nice in that they offer a natural look and feel, and they come in many different dimensions.

Wood is also great for chewing—don't be angry with your African Grey when he chews his wooden perches—this just means that he appreciates them. You can use "green" wood from trimmed trees from your backyard as perches, but you must make sure first that the tree is nontoxic and that it has not been sprayed with fertilizer or pesticides.

Concrete

Concrete perches are a necessity for your African Grey, as he will use them to keep his nails and beak trim. Offer two concrete perches of different dimensions, but be sure that these aren't the only perches you offer, because they can be irritating to the feet. African Greys will often choose to sleep on a concrete perch because it offers good footing. A concrete perch might also be used as a "napkin" after a particularly messy meal, so clean and disinfect it regularly.

Rope

Rope perches are fun to play with and come in a variety of dimensions and colors. They can be twisted into all kinds of shapes to fit in your African Grey's cage. Your African Grey will have a ball shredding the rope, but you must make sure to check it every few days for loose strands which can wrap around a leg or neck and cause serious injury—keep all ragged strands neatly trimmed.

Plastic

Plastic perches are easy to clean and are inexpensive, but they are not pleasant to stand on. Use a minimum amount of plastic perches and make sure that you provide other types of perches as well. Some acrylic perches come with toys attached, and these are a nice addition to the many perches you should offer.

Cups

The standard commercial cage usually comes with two square, plastic cups designed to fit neatly into doors located toward the bottom of the cage. These cups are, by no means, the best choice for your African Grey. Plastic cups are difficult to clean, not only because the square shape does not allow thorough cleaning of the crevices, but because the plastic eventually becomes scratched, and bacteria like to hide out in the scratches and muck up the water. A standard cage usually has places for the cups at the lower half of the cage, which might allow wastes to fall into the cups—not sanitary at all. Plastic cups also tend to break, and they are lightweight enough for a busy African Grey to turn over and dump the contents.

Replace plastic cups with three pairs of round, stainless-steel cups—two for water, two for seed/pellets, and two for fresh foods, though you will only use one set at a time, allowing the other set to be thoroughly washed and dried before its next use. Stainless steel

Offer your Grey heavy, sturdy cups made of ceramic or stainless steel. These are easy to clean, and your Grey can't easily dump their contents.

is easy to clean and is very durable. Ceramic cups are nice as well, but they are easier to break and will eventually scratch. Many stainless steel or ceramic cups come with no-dump holders, so you won't have to worry about spillage. African Greys are notorious for dumping cups, so you might want to consider a locked-on, hooded cup that will help prevent mess.

Some people use water bottles or self-watering tubes to dispense water. These have the disadvantage of becoming clogged or dirty, and owners tend to refresh the water less frequently. A coop cup filled with clean water at least twice a day should do nicely—no need for bottles or tubes.

Toys

Toys are a must for the high-energy, busy African Grey—an African Grey without toys to fling, chew, snuggle, and argue with will be bored and unhappy. Toys give your Grey something to do while you're away and offer much-needed exercise to a cage-bound bird. Greys actually develop relationships with their toys, so watch for your bird's interactions with his different toys—this can be very amusing.

"Safety first" is the motto when it comes to toys for your African Grey. Beware of toys that are flimsy or have small spaces that can catch a toe. Your bird's head should never be able to fit in a ring that

Toys are necessary for the intelligent, high-energy African Grey, and it is a good idea to rotate his toys from week to week to keep him interested.

comes on a toy. Never consider offering toys that are made for much larger or much smaller birds.

Soft wooden toys, often combined with leather, hard treats, and lava rocks are a great choice for the African Grey, and he will enjoy chewing the wood. Make certain that all colored wood is made with natural dye—the toy should indicate the type of dye on its label.

Tough acrylic toys are great, but plastic toys made for parakeets are not wise choices—your African Grey has a powerful beak and can break these easily. Toys with bells will be especially appreciated, but make sure that the clappers are firmly attached or your bird might swallow them. Jingle-type bells are not appropriate for African Greys, as they might catch a beak or toe caught in the small opening and become seriously injured as a result.

Preening toys or those that contain rope, sisal, feathers, or floss are fun, especially for the single African Grey, as he will enjoy having something to preen other than himself. Be careful, however, with fraying rope toys—make sure you keep all loose strands neatly trimmed.

African Greys like swings, so make sure that you provide your pet with at least one. Some swings come with toys or beads attached, adding extra things for your African Grey to do. Homemade toys are great when used with supervision. Toilet paper rolls cut into rings and hung on sisal rope are very entertaining, as are shredded, blank newsprints tied into small bundles. A whole roll of toilet paper can be very entertaining for a Grey, but you'll have to clean up the mess.

Rotating your African Grey's toys is a great way to keep them "new" and allow you time to clean them. Buy more toys than will fit in the cage at any one time and rotate them in and out of the cage on a weekly basis. Don't remove your African Grey's absolute favorite toys, however, as this can cause undue stress. If you notice that your Grey becomes anxious when you change the accessories in his cage, discontinue the practice. Greys like consistency and may not appreciate a lot of fussing around with their cages.

Other Accessories

Now that you've taken care of the essential cage accessories, there are other indispensable items that your African Grey will need to thrive.

Bird Lamp

If you live in a northern climate that is dark for much of the year, or if your African Grey lives in a room that doesn't get much light, you should invest in a bird lamp. There are many available on the market, or you can simply buy a spotlight from a hardware store and equip it with a bird or reptile bulb from your local pet store. This high-spectrum bulb provides your African Grey with the "natural" light he needs to maintain its health. A bird kept without the proper light can become malnourished, or at least very stressed. You can keep the light on for nine to ten hours a day.

Cage Cover

Your African Grey does not need his cage covered at night, though people who like to sleep a little later in the morning might do well to invest in a dark cage cover. A cover also serves to keep out drafts.

Don't use the cover, however, for extended periods of time in daylight hours—it should only be used for a few minutes to calm a raucous bird in the event that you need him to be silent, such as when an infant is taking a nap. Be careful that the cover does not have holes become frayed, both of which can injure or kill an African Grey. Make sure that covering your Grey doesn't stress him out, which can lead to unwanted behaviors.

Nightlight

If your bird becomes frightened at night or if you have a cat or rodents roaming the house, you will want to keep a nightlight on in your bird room. This will give your African Grey a sense of security—he will be able to tell the difference between a real predator and someone making a midnight snack in the kitchen.

Cage Locks

Most African Greys are quite proficient at escaping from their cages. Invest in spring clips or another type of lock and keep them on the doors at all times. An African Grey can easily break a flimsy lock, so be sure to invest in sturdy locks.

Mineral Block and Cuttlebone

These items provide much-needed calcium to your African Grey's diet and are fun to chew and destroy. Make sure that your bird has at least one of each, and replace them when they become soiled or consumed.

Birdy Kabob

A birdy kabob is a metal stick on to which you thread all kinds of goodies, such as fresh fruits and vegetables. The stick is usually capped on the end so that there's no sharp point. The kabob mimics eating behavior in the wild and makes your African Grey exert some energy to get his food. You can also use the kabob to thread paper and other fun items with which your bird will like to play.

Flooring

Your African Grey's cage should have a metal grating on the bottom so that he can't get to his mess, but you will need to put something in the bottom of the cage nonetheless. Regular newspaper is by far the easiest choice, and if you change it at least every other day, it's sanitary as well. Many people use corncob or other types of litter for the cage bottom, but these tend to hold moisture and might be cleaned less frequently because they often don't look dirty when they really are.

Bath

Most Greys do not like to bathe, but some will do so in the water dish. If you notice that your bird likes to bathe, you can provide a shallow bath a few times a week. A mister or spray bottle is a good way to bathe the reluctant Grey.

Play Gym

A play gym is an exercise stand for birds. Your African Grey will appreciate a cage-top play gym, complete with ladders, toys, and even a cup for snacks. African Greys can be easily trained to stay put on a play gym, especially if it offers interesting activities.

Bird Harness

The bird harness is a relatively new item in the pet trade and is a better choice than the leg chain, which can lead to a broken leg or foot. The harness looks like a dog or cat harness and fits around your bird's body, under his wings. Most African Greys will not stand being strapped into this item and may become irritated or try to chew it off, unless they are conditioned to accept the harness when

Play gyms provide hours of entertainment for your Grey, complete with ladders, toys, and other obstacles.

Cage-top play gyms are a favorite with Greys and can aid in training your bird.

they are very young. This harness will prevent your bird from flying away, but so will outdoor safety measures. Never take your bird outside unless its wings are well clipped and you are certain that you will be with him every second.

Seed Catchers

African Greys are messy creatures. A commercial seed guard attached to the cage will go a long way toward keeping the seed inside the cage. A flimsy plastic guard is easily destroyed and inappropriate for a Grey.

Mite Protectors

You will find mite protectors for sale in most pet shops, but there is no need for this item. In fact, the chemicals inside can be harmful for your bird. Instead of the mite protector, take your bird to the veterinarian for a checkup. It's unlikely that your African Grey has mites or will ever contract them.

SETTING UP THE CAGE

You now have what seems like far more cage accessories than a bird needs! But take heart, however, because your African Grey will use and appreciate all of these essential items—provided they are set up properly in his cage. The following is a cage setup checklist to help you place everything appropriately.

1. Make sure that all of the parts of the cage are put together correctly and securely.
2. Place full food and water cups toward the front of the cage and about midway to the top. If the doors where the cups should go are too low, don't use them—use a cup holder instead.
3. Place perches at various levels toward the middle to the top of the cage, making sure that there are no perches above food or water dishes. African Greys prefer to be at a high point in the cage, so don't position perches too low. If you place perches above one another, realize that they are going to become soiled.
4. Place the cuttlebone and mineral block on the sides of the cage near a perch. Don't place these items too low, where they can be soiled.
5. Place toys in various spots around the cage, making sure that they don't block the food and water dishes.
6. Pull out tray and add newspaper to the bottom of the cage below the grate.
7. Add a Grey bird.
8. Place the spring clips or locks on the doors.

When setting up your Grey's cage, place perches toward the middle and the top of the cage, making sure there are no food or water dishes below the perches.

You're done! Your African Grey is home!

CLEANING YOUR AFRICAN GREY'S CAGE

When you have an African Grey, expect to do a good deal of cleaning. The smart African Grey owner invests in a good handheld vacuum. Daily cleaning chores include changing the paper in the bottom of the cage (you can do this every other day, if you're pressed for time), soaking the dishes (you should have two sets) in a 10-percent bleach solution, making sure there are no wastes deposited on the perches, and rinsing the cups thoroughly before using them.

Weekly chores include disassembling the cage (if it's small enough) and cleaning it thoroughly with a bleach solution or kitchen soap and a scrub brush, scrubbing all the perches, and cleaning and rotating toys. A larger cage can be hosed down outside—remove your bird first, of course.

Many household detergents and cleansers are extremely dangerous for your African Grey. Instead, use vinegar as a disinfectant and baking soda as a cleanser. Don't mix the two, however. A 10-percent bleach solution is fine as well—bleach is nontoxic to birds. Of course, make sure you rinse everything thoroughly before putting your African Grey back in the newly cleaned cage.

FEEDING Your African Grey Parrot

We know much more about birds and their nutritional needs than we did even 15 years ago—in fact, there's a lot of emphasis placed on good avian nutrition these days. At one time, many people assumed that fulfilling an African Grey's dietary needs only required feeding him seeds and changing his water. However, we now know that this diet can actually be compared to feeding a prisoner solely bread and water. Not only is an all-seed diet unhealthy, but it will barely sustain an African Grey, much less allow him to thrive.

With all of the new avian food products available today, feeding your African Grey the right foods can seem a little confusing. There are so many different products on the market—seed mixes, pellets, supplements, treats—where should you begin? This chapter shows you a simple way to feed your African Grey properly and how to get the most nutrition out of the foods you offer.

AN AFRICAN GREY'S BASIC DIET

Like humans, African Grey Parrots need a healthy, balanced diet in order to receive their proper nutrition. Pellets offer many nutrients, and fruits and vegetables are absolutely necessary for an African Grey's diet. Seeds are not all bad either—even though feeding an all-seed diet is deadly for any species of African Grey, a diet that

Greys need a nutritious, balanced diet—not just seeds—in order to thrive and stay healthy.

offers other, more nutritious items in addition to seed can actually be a healthy, balanced diet. The following section outlines what should constitute an African Grey's basic diet and what role each of these foods plays toward fulfilling your bird's complete dietary needs.

Pellets

Some manufacturers produce a pelleted diet, which consists of nuggets into which all of the nutrients your African Grey needs are supposedly compacted. Though pelleted diets do provide many of the nutrients Greys need, they should not be considered a nutritionally complete meal.

Pellets are relatively new on the scene for parrot-type birds, having been originally used only for poultry. The research conducted on poultry nutrition far exceeds the research done on parrot nutrition, and the life of the average pet bird far exceeds that of a chicken raised for food. Not much is known on the long-term effects of birds eating these manufactured diets.

Furthermore, a pellet prepared for an African Grey is also the same pellet prepared for Amazon Parrots, Cockatoos, and Macaws of all sizes and species, even though their dietary needs may be very different. How can it be that these very dissimilar birds can thrive on the same formula? Their metabolisms are different, their needs for certain nutrients are different, and their activity levels and propensities toward obesity are different as well. There is also evidence that some of these diets can promote liver and kidney disease.

Some avian experts highly recommend the use of these pellets as the bird's staple food, suggesting that the bird need only eat these nuggets and nothing else. For the active, curious African Grey, this is a very boring proposition.

However, all of this does not mean that you shouldn't feed pellets. Pellets can be a nutritious, fun addition to your African Grey's diet, and your avian veterinarian may, indeed, suggest pellets as the staple food in your bird's diet. Offer pellets in conjunction with all of the other foods you feed—variety in a bird's diet is the key to good health. Pellets are also a great addition to many bird-specific recipes and add a lot of nourishment to the cooked foods you offer your African Grey.

Ultimately, your avian veterinarian should be the one to determine the correct diet for your individual bird. If your bird's doctor believes that pellets are the proper base diet, then you can consider making the switch to pellets, but do your research on the dietary needs of your species before you make the switch.

Seeds

Seed is fatty and doesn't have all the nutrients that your African Grey requires to remain healthy. In fact, an African Grey eating only seed will begin to suffer from various maladies and can eventually die of them. African Greys can live from 40 to 50 years, but an African Grey on a primarily seed diet might only live only 10 years or less. A small amount of seed, in addition to a diet filled with healthy foods, is an acceptable base diet.

You will find seed labeled for African Greys or large birds at your pet store—this is the correct mix to feed your African Grey. You can feed an inxpensive mix if you notice that your African Grey enjoys it—these mixes often contain dried fruit and nuts that are fun for your African Grey to snack on. Remember, however, that seeds are not *all* you are going to feed your African Grey.

Keep seeds in an airtight container or in the refrigerator or freezer so that they do not become contaminated with seed flies. Use a clean scoop to dole out the seed instead of dipping your bird's contaminated dish into it.

Seed mixes are acceptable in small amounts, but other fresh and healthy foods should make up the bulk of your Grey's diet.

Corn is a delicious fun-to-eat food that you can offer to your Grey as a treat.

Switching from Seeds to Pellets

If your veterinarian advises you to switch to a pelleted diet, you can't simply discontinue seed and expect your African Grey to know that the pellets are food. You might inadvertently starve your bird by making him go "cold turkey." Instead, begin mixing the seeds and the pellets at a 50/50 ratio for a week. The next week, mix the seeds at a 40/60 ratio and so on, until the bowl is only filled with pellets. This may take at least a month.

During this time, you should weigh your African Grey to ensure that he is not losing too much weight, and you should carefully watch to make sure that he is actually eating the pellets. Continue feeding other fresh and cooked foods as well.

Vegetables and Fruits

Vegetables are an important part of your African Grey's diet, offering a variety of nutrients that your African Grey needs to survive. Fruit is important as well. Most fruits are full of sugar and can be fattening, but they are also so rich in nutrients that they are worth the calories.

The following is a list of vegetables and fruits that you can offer every day. Items like corn and celery are not as nutritious, but they are fun to eat and make a good once-in-a-while treat. Remember, variety is key—offer as many as you can of these items daily.

Vegetables

Asparagus
Beet tops
Beets (raw or cooked)
Broccoli
Brussels sprouts
Carrots (raw or cooked)
Celery
Chard
Collard Greens
Corn
Dandelion
Endive
Green beans
Green peppers
Jalapenos
Kale
Mustard greens
Peas
Pumpkin
Red peppers
Spinach
Watercress
Yams (cooked)
Yellow peppers
Yellow squash
Zucchini

Fruits

Apples
Apricots
Bananas
Berries
Cantaloupe
Cherries
Figs
Grapefruit
Grapes
Honeydew
Kiwi
Mango
Oranges
Papaya
Peaches
Pears
Pineapple
Plums
Watermelon

Make sure to remove all fruit within a few hours of feeding it to your bird—fruit can spoil or attract fruit flies, pesky little flying bugs that are tough to get rid of once they've made an appearance. Cooked veggies should also be removed within a few hours, especially if you live in a warm climate.

Table Foods

Your African Grey can eat just about anything that you eat. The more healthy table foods you can get your African Grey to eat, the better. With the exception of chocolate, avocado, rhubarb, alcohol, and salty, sugary, and fatty foods, your bird can eat everything on your plate.

Vegetables are a necessary part of your African Grey's diet—your bird needs the nutrients they provide to survive.

Fruits, such as bananas and grapes, are rich in nutrients your Grey needs, but make sure you regulate your bird's intake of these sugary foods.

Share your meals and be persistent if your bird is reluctant to try new foods—simply keep offering them, and your bird's curiosity will get the best of him. It might seem like cannibalism, but your African Grey might even enjoy turkey or chicken and will even hold and gnaw on a chicken bone. Don't forget to bring a "birdy bag" home with you when you go out to eat.

Snacks

The love we feel for our birds is often expressed with treats: seed sticks, seed balls, seed, seed, seed. Too much of a good thing is still too much. Limit seed treats to once a week. As an alternative, treat your African Grey to a special type of fruit or other healthy snack— this will prevent your bird from gorging on "candy" and keep his appetite fresh for more nutritious foods. Don't give up on treats, though—your African Grey may enjoy the occasional sweet seed stick.

Healthy, low-fat snacks include air-popped popcorn, healthy cereal, whole-wheat crackers (spread with peanut butter for the occasional sticky treat), and whole-wheat bread. Nuts in the shell, such as almonds and filberts, are a good snack for an African Grey, who has to "work" to get at the meat, but most nuts are fatty and should be fed sparingly. Peanuts are supposed to contain a toxin that is harmful to birds in large doses, so be wary of seed-mixes that contain a lot of peanuts.

Commercially Prepared Diets

Several companies now make dry diets that you can cook for your Grey. These are nutritious and are usually relished by Greys because they like to eat warm, soft foods. You can even cook them with fresh juices instead of water and add veggies to make them even more nutritious. I cook for my Grey every day, and he looks forward to his warm meal.

Homemade Recipes

Cooking food for your African Grey is a great way to provide nutritious, safe, fun foods. The following are a few recipes that you can try. You can freeze portions of each of these and thaw each day for a new, fresh treat. All of these recipes are easy and very variable—you can add whatever you happen to have in the kitchen as long as it is safe.

African Grey Bread

Buy a package of corn muffin mix and follow the directions on the package. When you have the batter mixed, add $^1/_2$ cup pellets, $^1/_2$ cup dried fruit, $^1/_2$ cup canned beans (any kind), $^1/_2$ cup broccoli (or other veggie), 2 Tbs. of crushed cuttlebone, 2 Tbs. chunky peanut butter, and anything else you think your African Grey might like. Bake until a knife comes out clean from the center of the bread. This may take far longer to cook than the package recommends.

African Grey Pancakes

Make pancake batter the way you normally would (if you're like me, use instant) and add 1 cup pellets, $^1/_4$ cup dried apricots, and $^1/_4$ cup shredded carrots. Make these the same way you would make regular pancakes. You can add anything else to the batter you think your African Grey might like.

African Grey Omelet

Crack several eggs into a bowl, including the shells, and add pellets, two types of chopped veggies, dried fruit, and anything else your African Grey will like. Cook as you would for any omelet or scramble. Cool extremely well. Freeze and thaw a small portion each day.

African Grey Pasta

Boil whole-wheat pasta and drain. Pour it in a saucepan and melt soy cheese over it. Add pellets, veggies, bananas, crushed hardboiled egg (including shell), or whatever else your African Grey likes. You can freeze this in ice cube trays and defrost a cube a day. Makes a nutritious and colorful treat!

African Grey Beans and Rice

This recipe is very easy. Simply soak and boil beans, any type. You can use canned beans if that's easier for you. Cook brown rice and mix it in with the beans. Grate a couple of carrots into the mixture and toss in three or four chopped jalapeno peppers. Freeze in ice cube trays and pop one cube out each day. Thaw before serving.

The Dangers of Nonstick Cookware and Appliances

If you decide to cook these recipes for your Grey, remember to *never* cook using nonstick cookware if your bird lives in the house. Non-stick cookware has a special coating, and this coating emits a colorless, odorless fume when heated that kills birds almost immediately.

Nonstick coating can be found on griddles, pans, deep fryers, bread makers, crock pots, and many other kitchen utensils and appliances. To cook safely, use only cookware made of stainless steel, copper, or other materials that do not have nonstick coating present.

Dietary Supplements

Some African Grey owners add supplements to their birds' diets. Common supplements include cuttlebone, mineral block, and calcium powder, especially for the Grey, because he seems to need more calcium than most other birds. The Grey's bones are dense, and he needs a consistent supply of calcium to maintain proper health. Some Greys become calcium-deficient and can have seizures and bone fractures. Foods that are high in calcium, such as almonds, kale, and small amounts of dairy products (cheese, yogurt, etc.) are the best sources of this important nutrient.

Some people drizzle supplemental oils over their birds' seeds and sprinkle supplement powder on top of that. This is not harmful for an African Grey, and can even enhance the diet. Consult your

Some owners offer their Greys calcium supplements to keep them healthy. However, consult your veterinarian before adding supplements to your Grey's diet.

veterinarian before you begin to supplement your African Grey's diet. An African Grey that relishes produce, table foods, and pellets, and eats a small amount of seed should not require a supplement.

The supplement grit that you will find in pet stores is not recommended for African Greys. They do not really need it and may gorge on it and become very ill and even die as a result.

Fresh Water

Clean, fresh water is essential to your African Grey's well-being. You should offer bottled or filtered water only and make sure that you refresh it at least twice a day. African Greys are notorious for making soup, tossing everything into their water for a nice soak. This can cause bacteria to flourish and will make your bird ill if he drinks this nasty concoction. Adding a drop or two of apple cider vinegar to your African Grey's water will help retard the growth of bacteria and is healthful for your bird as well.

Supplementing the water with vitamins is not always recommended because the vitamins provide bacteria with nutrients for spawning, turning your bird's water into a slimy mess unless you use a water cleanser. I sometimes use water cleanser, apple cider vinegar, a powdered vitamin supplement, and/or a calcium supplement in my Grey's water, but not all of these things every day. Some days he gets just plain, clear, clean water.

Your African Grey's water dish should be clean enough for you to drink from. You should also have two sets of water dishes—the one in use and one soaking in a bleach solution and drying for use the next day. Water bottles not only tend to become clogged, but they also harbor bacteria in the tube and are more difficult to clean. Owners also tend to change the water in them less frequently as well. Instead, use a stainless steel coop cup for water—your African Grey may try to bathe in it and toss its food inside the cup, but that's what African Greys do—you'll just have to clean it more often. The bonus to that is that your Grey will always have fresh water.

PUTTING IT ALL TOGETHER: A TOTAL FEEDING PLAN

Now that you know all of the types of foods that are necessary for meeting your African Grey's nutritional needs, you need to know how much and how often you should offer these foods—and when to feed them.

Morning Meal

Birds generally feed in the morning, when they are hungriest, and in the evening, a few hours before the sun goes down, though

The morning feeding should include lots of fresh fruits, vegetables, and healthy cooked foods as well.

most of our companion birds tend to feed all day, a habit that can lead to obesity and other health issues. The morning feeding should consist of a bounty of fresh foods: sprouted seeds and beans, carrots, spinach, apple, squash, grapes, melon, kale, broccoli, and any other fresh food your bird loves to eat. Make sure that you provide at least four different fresh foods daily and offer them in abundance. Vegetables and fruits that are very dark-green or orange are especially good—you may have to experiment with a variety of foods before you know what your African Grey likes.

Offer healthy cooked foods at this time as well, especially if you have made them with your bird in mind. Sprouts and sprouted beans are a very important part of the morning meal, so be sure that you offer them at least three times a week. You can sprout your own seeds and beans or buy them from a heath food store. A "birdy kabob" is a great way to serve veggies and fruit. Simply thread the food onto the kabob and hang it in the cage—this gives your bird the illusion of eating food in the wild, making him "work" for his meal.

You don't have to remove the seed dish for this morning feeding—your bird is allowed to pick at the remaining seeds from the night before. Make sure that this meal is hardy—you want to feed a wide variety of foods, including starchy foods, such as sweet potatos, bananas, and whole-wheat bread.

Midday Meal

The next meal, a few hours later or in the late afternoon, should consist of pellets, cooked foods, and other healthy foods your African Grey loves. Remove the fresh foods (always remove fresh foods before they begin to spoil) and offer the other foods, along with a bowl of pellets, if you choose to use them. Some African Greys are reluctant to eat pellets, but if you begin serving them when your African Grey is a youngster, there is a good probability that your bird will eat them.

Make sure that your African Grey is eating what you offer at this meal, because you don't want him to go hungry for a good portion of the day. If you don't want to serve pellets, serve a cooked rice and bean mix at this time—your Grey will love it.

Evening Meal

The final meal, given in the late afternoon or evening, should

The evening meal should consist of a protein source, fruits, vegetables, and a good seed mix.

consist of a protein source—a very well-done hardboiled egg, some boiled or grilled chicken, or something from your dinner plate. Offer favorite veggies and fruits as well, whole-wheat bread, sprouts, and a bowl of a good seed mix.

Most people work all day and can't provide food all day long. That's okay—simply combine the meals, offering one before you go to work and one when you come home in the evening, around dinnertime. This system provides your African Grey with fresh produce, seeds, pellets, table foods, and foods cooked especially for him—a very balanced diet. Make sure, however, that your African Grey has food that he likes available at all times—you never want to starve your bird.

INTRODUCING NEW FOODS

You will find that your African Grey chooses a couple of favorite foods and will often exclude other foods in order to eat these favorites. This is great if those foods are healthy and nutritious. For example, if your African Grey's favorite foods are squash, carrots, and red peppers, you can feel free to feed them every day. If your bird's favorite foods are seed, celery, and watermelon, you might want to begin limiting those foods and offering more nutritious options—but that does not mean you have to exclude those favorites completely. Just make sure you can get him to eat other nutritious foods as well.

One way to do this is to introduce new, healthy foods. Most likely, he will view the change as something novel and interesting while getting some extra nutrients at the same time. Offer new foods gradually and show your bird that they are good by nibbling on them yourself. You can't force an African Grey to gorge on something he doesn't recognize as food, such as snow peas or a slice of melon, but if you keep offering it, day after day, the bird will eventually check out the new item.

Some owners become frustrated with their birds because the bird refuses a food item for several days. It can take up to two weeks or more for a bird to begin to nibble at a new food, so if you are determined that your African Grey try carrots, keep offering the carrots every day, even if it seems like a waste of time and carrots. You can even try to offer foods in different ways—for example, raw carrots, grated carrots, steamed sliced carrots, mashed carrots, carrots baked into muffins, and so on. Eating the carrot yourself and offering it to a family member and praising the person for eating it will entice your Grey to try the new item.

EXERCISE AND NUTRITION

No discussion of nutrition would be complete without a note on exercise. You know that if you eat a completely healthy diet but get no exercise, you will not become fit and trim. The same goes for your African Grey. If your bird is housed in a very large cage or aviary and is allowed to fly, you can be assured that he is getting the exercise he needs—flying is the best form of exercise for a bird.

If your African Grey lives in a small cage or has his wings clipped, you should make sure that he gets the exercise he needs to remain healthy and fit. Simply clambering around a cage is not sufficient exercise for an African Grey; you have to play with your pet in an active way, too. You can place him at the bottom of a rope or bird ladder and have him climb up. Even a clipped African Grey enjoys a good wing flapping session and will appreciate being out of the cage so that he can flap away without hitting a toy or the bars of his cage.

A NOTE ON CONSISTENCY

It is important to be consistent with feeding your African Grey healthy foods all of the time, not just in the beginning or when it's convenient. Some bird owners become very enthusiastic about their bird's diet for the first few months, making sure it contains everything he needs. Eventually, this enthusiasm wanes, and these birds are once again receiving an unbalanced diet, which they quickly get used to eating. It may be difficult, after a period of time, to get your African Grey to eat properly again, so you want to make sure to feed a healthy diet that you can maintain. This might mean preparing foods in advance and keeping them in the freezer or chopping veggies the night before you feed them—but all of this effort is worth it when you realize that you're doing something essential for the health of your bird.

BEHAVIOR of the African Grey

Greys are expressive birds. An African Grey will let a guardian know what he wants and needs and when he's happy or unhappy, and this enables a person to effectively communicate with his or her African Grey. However, you have to get to know your bird before you can come to recognize how he behaves when he's feeling a certain way. It's the same as getting to know another person—you have to pay attention.

A domestic animal is one that humans have changed through selective breeding to suit our needs. Dogs, for example, are bred to accomplish certain tasks, such as herding or hunting rodents. Companion birds, on the other hand, have not been changed so drastically that they have lost their natural instincts. We can understand why a Border Collie herds sheep, but we have a difficult time understanding why an African Grey wants to chew the wallpaper—this behavior seems to serve no purpose.

The African Grey is an animal that acts out of pure instinct. He does not do things to spite you (well, not always!), nor does he do things to assist you. He merely acts out of a desire to fulfill his natural urges, whether that be chewing, screaming, or cuddling. The African Grey, in general, is an energetic, bold, sensitive creature that is at once loyal and territorial, and his normal behaviors can often seem bewildering to an owner who is not used to observing this unique companion. This chapter will help to take some of the confusion out of why African Greys behave the way they do.

AFRICAN GREY INTELLIGENCE

The African Grey is a very clever creature, able to learn to do things all on his own, like opening a cage door to escape or dumping a water dish for attention. Do not underestimate the brainpower of this bird. The African Grey will learn things all by himself and will even find ways to manipulate his owner to get attention. Tenacity and self-direction are part of the African Grey's charm, and the superior intelligence of this bird definitely contributes to his behaviors.

Research on African Greys has shown that they are able to understand far more than anyone previously imagined a bird could

Most African Greys frequently vocalize and are wonderful at mimicking sounds that humans make.

learn. African Greys are able to recognize words and associate them with objects the same way humans do. African Greys may even understand what their owners are saying and might not be mimicking at all, but actually talking and communicating in a language that isn't even theirs. Research suggests that African Greys have the intelligence of a four-year-old human child and the emotional capacity of a two-year-old human.

VOCALIZATION

A healthy African Grey will be vocal around dawn and again around dusk. In the wild, dawn is the time when African Greys are calling to one another to say, "I've made it through the night." At dusk, they call one another again to say, "Here's where I've settled to roost. I'm okay." At these times you will hear your African Grey babbling, whistling, talking, and making other noises. Your bird might call to you at these times and will appreciate an answer—you should call back with "I'm here, everything's okay," or your bird's name. This will help your African Grey feel secure. These vocalizations are called "contact calling" and are completely normal. African Greys will also vocalize during the day for various reasons, perhaps to call you to play, warn you of potential perceived danger, or to request some food or water.

If you are not a fan of getting up at dawn on a daily basis, you can regulate what time your African Grey begins to vocalize by regulating the amount of light that hits the cage. You can do this by covering the cage at night and uncovering it at a desired time in the morning. You can also draw dark curtains over your windows or have a separate sleeping cage in another, darker room to achieve the same effect. This cage is not for punishment or anything else, just for sleep.

Mimicking and "Talking"

African Greys are wonderful at mimicking sounds that humans make. This behavior is the African Grey's attempting to connect with his "flock" and indicates that the bird is attached to his human family or is at least paying attention to his surroundings. An African Grey will often associate sounds with speech. For example, an African Grey might say, "Hello" when the phone rings, because that's what he hears humans doing. Some African Greys are better talkers than others, though most will pick up words and phrases, and all of them seem to enjoy whistling.

Most Greys will begin to speak at around one year of age, though some will speak much sooner, and some not at all. The precursor to actually forming words is "baby babbling," sounds similar to the noises a human baby makes when trying the language out for the first time. This babbling is a Grey's way of testing his mimicking ability—it means that actual words are not too far behind.

If your Grey regularly "talks," he is probably trying to communicate with his human family, or he is simply very responsive to his surroundings.

If your Grey picks up an annoying or loud noise, you may be able to stop it in the early stages by not responding to the noise. If the noise persists, you can try to replace the noise with something more pleasing. For example, every time your bird makes the noise, you can say something you would prefer to hear to another person and reward the person with lavish verbal praise when he or she says it back. Your Grey will soon come to see that his annoying noise doesn't get a reward but that the phrase the other person is mimicking does, and he may pick up the better phrase in order to get attention. If there's no one around to play mimic, you can say the preferred word to a stuffed animal and then praise it—the Grey will wonder what all the fuss is about and pick up the word so that he can get some praise, too.

NORMAL BEHAVIORS

African Greys can do some pretty uncanny things that look like problem behaviors, but many of these behaviors are actually quite healthy and normal. You can also tell a lot about how an African Grey feels by observing his body language—it is usually a great indicator of what your bird is thinking and feeling at that moment.

By observing your Grey's body language, you can discover a great deal about what your bird is thinking and feeling at any given time.

This section outlines many of the behaviors that are normal for African Greys and why your bird exhibits these behaviors.

Preening

Preening is when your African Grey runs his beak through his feathers, making sure they are all clean and in place. Each feather is made up of little strands that zip together like Velcro; your African Grey spends a lot of time making sure that each feather is zipped properly. This isn't for vanity purposes: clean feathers are good insulators and allow a bird to fly properly.

Beak Grinding

When an African Grey is sleepy and content, he will audibly grind the two parts of his beak together. Experts cannot find a distinct reason for this; parrots seem to do it simply because they want to.

Beak Wiping

When an African Grey eats a particularly juicy or messy meal, he will wipe his beak along the sides of his cage or on a perch, usually the concrete conditioning perch if one is provided. This is akin to a human wiping his or her face with a napkin and is one reason why it's a good idea to disinfect and scrub perches weekly.

Beaking

African Greys "beak" a lot, meaning they use their beak to feel out things. "Beaking" is different from biting in that beaking is simply a way to discover the properties of something, the way we do with our hands.

An African Grey explores his world using his beak. A baby African Grey will use his beak to test the solidness of a perch—or of your hand. Do not be afraid of your baby African Grey's beak; the bird might just be trying to determine if your hand is a safe place to stand. Beaking is also a way that birds show affection.

If your African Grey's beaking becomes too forceful and hurts you (feels more like a bite), simply tell your bird, "No," remove your hand slowly, and walk away for a moment. Never whip your hand away and make a big scene. You may inadvertently teach your African Grey that hard beaking or biting is fun.

Head Shaking

Greys frequently shake their heads as if there was water in their ears. This is normal and does not indicate a head or ear problem.

Wing Flapping

Wing flapping while standing on a perch provides much needed exercise for a clipped bird. A bird that's flapping his wings might be testing out newly grown in feathers.

"Beaking" is a normal Grey behavior—Greys use their beaks to feel things out and to explore the world.

Flattened Posture, Wings Shaking

This posture means that your African Grey desperately wants something or wants to go somewhere. He is ready to take action, which may mean launching himself toward the object he wants—maybe you!

Regurgitation

As unpleasant as it sounds, an African Grey that is bobbing his head in your direction may be "affectionately" regurgitating to you. This is a high compliment. An African Grey will rarely vomit on you—it's the thought that counts more in this case.

Head Down, Neck Feathers Ruffled

An African Grey that is very bonded to you might desire a good bit of head and neck scratching and will show you this by putting his head down for you and offering you a fluffed neck. Gently rub your bird against the feathers and circle the ear openings lightly. If this causes your African Grey to yawn, then you know you're doing it right!

Chewing

African Greys love to chew, and this is a normal behavior. Don't consider it an aggressive act if your African Grey chews your

Many African Greys enjoy a neck or head scratch; your bird will indicate this to you by putting his neck down with his neck feathers ruffled.

Chewing is a natural, instinctual behavior for African Greys, so provide your Grey with plenty of toys and items he is allowed to chew on.

belongings to bits—he's just doing what his instincts tell him to do. If you want to save your priceless antiques, provide your bird with plenty of things to chew, including store bought toys and household items, such as toilet paper rolls.

Digging

For some reason, African Greys like to dig and will do so in their cages or in other materials, such as a large houseplant. It's not really understood why these birds dig, but it might have to do with something relating to diet or nesting. Housing your Grey in a cage with a grating on the bottom should take care of this behavior.

Toy Aggression

African Greys like to toss around their toys, throwing them around the cage and treating them roughly. Your Grey might choose one toy that he takes on as an "enemy." This is normal and does not indicate a problem.

Sleeping on One Foot

This means that your African Grey is healthy and content. An African Grey sleeping on two feet may not be feeling well or may be too warm.

Sleeping with His Head on His Back

No, your Grey isn't possessed (though this sleeping position can look like something out of "The Exorcist"); he just likes to sleep with his head resting on his back or under a wing.

Feather Fluffing

A quick ruffle of the feathers signifies a content bird that is releasing tension and getting ready to perform another task, such as flying or moving to the water dish. An African Grey sitting on a perch with his feathers fluffed may not be feeling well or might be cold. If your African Grey is fluffed, backed into a corner, wings shaking and beak open, he's displaying territorial behavior. Watch your fingers—this is a bird that's going to bite!

Stretching

African Greys stretch for the same reasons we do: because it feels good, releases tension, and gets tired muscles moving again.

Yawning

Birds yawn to clear their nasal passages, just like we do. If you notice excessive yawning in your African Grey, a health problem might be present.

Tail Bobbing

An African Grey that has just exercised might have a bobbing tail. If your bird's tail is bobbing a lot while he's resting on a perch, a respiratory problem could be developing.

Tail Wag

A quick tail wag means, "Okay, I'm ready to go. What's next?"

PROBLEM BEHAVIORS

Because African Greys are not domestic animals and their lives in human homes are truly foreign experiences, your companion African Grey may acquire problem behaviors that can cause some concern in an owner who doesn't understand why the behaviors are happening or how to change them. The following section describes a few of the most common behavioral problems African Greys experience.

Biting

African Greys are strong-willed creatures and can go through a nippy, aggressive stage. An African Grey's beak is very powerful and sharp and can cause damage to soft human flesh. One way to prevent biting is to never react emotionally when it happens. Basically, biting should be ignored. If you make a huge fuss about a bite, your Grey may do it again just to see you jump up and down. If you are bitten and you unintentionally reinforce the behavior by reacting, your Grey might learn that biting is a fun game or another way to manipulate you. You should also remember to play gently to keep the bird tame—if you play rough, your African Grey will learn to be rough.

If your once-tame African Grey is biting, it's important to find out why. Are you scaring the bird in some way? Is he becoming territorial with his cage? Whatever the case, regular biting is unacceptable. If the bird is on your hand when he bites, you can use the "wiggle" technique—rotate your arm such that the bird loses balance slightly.

An African Grey's beak is very sharp and powerful. To prevent biting, offer your Grey plenty of toys, and do not reinforce biting by reacting emotionally if it happens.

Giving a biting African Grey a "time-out," just as you would a child having a tantrum, is also a good way to teach him that biting is not going to be tolerated. Simply remove the biting bird to a smaller "time-out" cage placed in a quiet corner. When the bird is in this cage, you should not interact with him but wait for him to calm down and compose himself for about five minutes.

Never hit a bird or flick or strike his beak in any way. A bird's beak is very sensitive, and flicking it with a fingernail can hurt, causing your bird to mistrust you. You can hold the upper part of an African Grey's beak slightly if he persists in biting. At the same time, say, "No!" though most birds will continue doing what they want to do anyway. An African Grey that continues to bite may not be feeling well, so look for signs of illness. Take your bird to the veterinarian if you suspect something is wrong. Perhaps the bird is molting if he is not in the mood for handling.

Excessive Screaming

African Greys are not loud birds in general, but a confined or unhappy African Grey can become unbearable with his persistent vocalizations. If you feel that your bird is screaming excessively, try to discover the reason. For example, he might not be getting enough out-of-cage time, or he might not have enough to do. Sometimes, when a new African Grey comes into the home, the family lavishes affection on him, only to become bored with him after a while. This African Grey will not understand why the attention has stopped and may take up screaming or making a lot of noise to try to get the attention back.

Ignoring annoying noises is the easiest way to make them go away. You will also have to replace the annoying noise with something more pleasant. Verbally praise noises that you like and ignore the ones you don't, and your Grey will eventually get the idea that the "good" sounds get attention and the "bad" sounds don't.

Growling

Greys use a terrible growling sound to ward off interlopers, usually when they are extremely fearful. Wild-caught or improperly socialized birds are more likely to growl than a well-adjusted handfed baby.

Territorial Display

Some mature African Greys can be territorial of their cages and

Time out of the cage and a lot of hands-on attention can help prevent your Grey from experiencing boredom or exhibiting any neurotic behaviors.

will defend them by charging and gnashing at anyone who comes close. Occasionally, a female will lay an egg on the bottom of the cage and defend it like a lion defending cubs, though sometimes the bird won't care for the egg at all. In the case of a female laying infertile eggs, simply remove the eggs (you may need a glove to do this) and the bird should go back to her old, sweet self—until the next egg is laid.

Self-Mutilation

When an African Grey is bored, confined, mistreated, has nutritional deficiencies, or has experienced a drastic change in his life or environment, he may begin to pick out his feathers or chew other parts of his body, resulting in bleeding and bald patches. This is a terrible state for an African Grey, because this bird uses self-mutilation as a last resort to distract himself from deplorable living circumstances. Sometimes, an African Grey that has an illness, such as a problem with his respiratory system, will pluck the feathers around the disturbed area. Plucking and other mutilating behaviors always need medical attention.

Neurotic Behaviors

Confined African Greys will often develop a neck-swaying dance that indicates neurosis. This dance looks "cute" to the layperson but shows that the African Grey has been confined or mistreated for some time. Greys can also develop compulsive behaviors, such as banging the beak repeatedly against the cage. Time out of the cage and lots of hands-on attention should help to prevent these behaviors.

ACCEPTING YOUR AFRICAN GREY'S BIRDY BEHAVIOR

Because they like to chew, vocalize, and bite (often in play or when cranky), African Greys present a real challenge to the first-time bird owner. Your African Grey will seem unpredictable at first, but once you have some experience observing him, you will be able to tell when he is going to do just about anything, from biting to eliminating. The key to owning an African Grey is deciding whether or not you can provide the proper care for this sensitive bird and whether you have the time, money, and patience to deal with his needs and quirks.

SOCIALIZING and Training Your African Grey

The African Grey is a bird that needs constant stimulation. Once this bird becomes bored or neglected, it is likely to begin self-mutilating or neurotic behaviors. This means that you must provide your pet with everything he needs to keep himself mentally stimulated. A Grey is not on the move all the time—he takes naps and has moments where he just wants to sit up high and watch the world go by. However, when he wants to play or use his brain, there should be plenty of activities available. Chances are, you would like to train your bird as well, and your African Grey will most likely respond positively to training activities as well.

SOCIAL INTERACTION

The Grey needs an owner with time to spare. A Grey that spends ten hours in his cage daily, only to come out for half and hour before dinner, will be an unhappy Grey. This is a bird that loves his flock, one that finds protection in numbers. Provide your bird with several hours of social interaction a day.

This does not mean that all of this time will be devoted to petting the Grey. You can take your bird around while you complete your

The African Grey needs constant mental stimulation. Make sure there are plenty of activities available for him when he wants to play or use his brain.

everyday routine. Place perches in various parts of your home and simply move your Grey around as you change rooms. Provide a play stand at the dinner table and allow your bird to eat with you. If you work on a computer, place a towel over your chair and allow your Grey to stand on the back of it. This type of interaction will keep your bird stimulated and feeling like part of the flock.

It will also help the bird to learn things he otherwise wouldn't while sitting in his cage. If you tell your bird what you're doing, like washing the dishes, for example, he will come to learn what that means. Say, "I'm washing the dishes," to your bird every time you wash them, and eventually your Grey may offer to do them for you!

HAND TAMING

African Greys are birds that need a lot of attention and socializing, so your pet will most likely respond well to being hand tamed. It is much easier to hand tame a young African Grey, but even older African Greys can be hand tamed with a little extra time and patience.

Most African Greys will respond well to being hand tamed and will enjoy the attention.

Young African Greys are the easiest to hand tame. Be sure to handle young Greys in a very gentle, calm manner, and spend time handling them every day.

Handling Young African Greys

Fortunately, young African Greys are easy to handle. They have not yet learned to bite and are apt to be gentle with you and willing to try new things. Handle your youngster every day. Cuddle and play with him. Stroke his neck and head feathers in the direction opposite of feather growth. Many African Greys enjoy being scratched on the head and neck.

If your young African Grey begins to nip at your hands and it hurts, even if the bird is just playing, cease interaction with the bird the instant he bites, walk away, and ignore him for a minute or so. Nips from a youngster may turn into hard biting when the bird gets a little older, so you want to show the bird that biting stops playtime. The downside to this method is that the bird may learn that biting makes you go away, which is what he may want. You'll have to determine your bird's individual temperament to use the proper training techniques.

Preventing bad behavior in a youngster will avoid you having to train the behavior out of him once he gets older. It is far easier to train a good behavior *into* a bird than it is to stop a bird from doing something he has gotten used to. Behaviors that are instilled the first year of an African Grey's life will last for the entire lifetime of the bird.

For this reason, always handle your African Grey in a very gentle manner. Playing rough will teach him to play rough, too, and may result in biting behaviors. Your African Grey needs several hours out of his cage daily, as much supervised time as you can give him.

Hand Taming an Older African Grey

If you have acquired a mature, untamed, or semi-tame African Grey, the taming and training process will take a bit of time, more so than with a youngster. Using a gentle, slow training method is always preferable with animals as sensitive as African Greys.

When you first bring your untamed African Grey home, you will want to give him a period of adjustment. Your bird will be stressed in his new situation. Do not consider taming him until he has settled into a routine and has come to know you and view you without scrambling for the back of the cage or attacking you through the bars. This may take a few weeks to more than a month.

Once your new African Grey is adjusted to your home, you can begin taming. You will first need to clip the bird's wings. An untamed African Grey with free flight may simply fly away from you and not return. Even if you eventually want to allow your bird to fly, you will have to clip the wings during the training period—the feathers will grow back in time.

Once the bird's wings are clipped, you can begin the taming process. See if your African Grey will come out of his cage on his own. If not, you can remove your bird out of his cage with a towel and hold him gently in the towel to prevent him from biting you. He may struggle, but continue to be calm and talk to him in a low, soothing voice. Be sure that you know how to properly hold your bird so that you don't injure him. You can use gloves if you feel they are absolutely necessary to protect your hands, but it is not recommended. Gloves are scary to a bird and will make the training process longer and perhaps even impossible.

Take the bird to a small room. A bathroom is ideal, but be sure to close the toilet lid and remove any dangerous items that may fall and break if the bird comes in contact with them. Sit on the floor and place the bird gently on top of a T-stand, holding him there for a moment before you let go.

If the bird flies off the stand, gather up the bird again and put him back. Repeat this action until the bird eventually stands for a moment on the stand. Remember to remain calm. The bird may not want to stay put in the first few sessions, but keep trying. You can do this twice a day for 20 minutes each session, but no more than that. You want to begin to build trust with the bird, not stress him out.

Once you've gotten your bird to stay on the stand, talk to him in a very calm voice and begin to move one hand slowly up the stand toward the bird. This may cause him to fly or climb off of the stand again, or he may attack you. No matter—simply try again. Little by little, session after session, move your hand slowly toward your bird until allows it to come very close. The idea here is that the bird should eventually allow contact with your hand. This may take quite a while, so be patient.

TRAINING YOUR AFRICAN GREY

African Greys are indeed "trainable" to do many behaviors. African Greys are fast learners and they are extremely self-directed. However, it's likely that your bird will actually train *you* more than you will train *him*. Like a three-year-old human child, an African Grey can be persistent enough to make you give in to whatever he wants. If your African Grey is begging to be let out of his cage with persistent beeping (like a fire alarm with dying batteries), and you open the cage, he will soon learn that this method works. A diligent owner can work to avoid these mistakes, though most owners are "softies" and give in to their African Grey's demands. (I often fall into that category!)

Some African Greys can be trained to perform complicated behaviors, such as dunking a whiffleball into a small hoop, rollerskating, and even housetraining. Most African Greys will talk as well and can be trained to talk on command. Some can even be taught to know what they are saying and can actually communicate with their human guardians. By training your African Grey, you can further develop your relationship with him, while at the same time providing interesting, challenging activities for him.

Positive Reinforcement

Positive reinforcement is the only way to encourage desired behaviors in your African Grey. When your bird does something that you want him to do, even if the behavior happened by accident, make a big scene about how great the behavior was and praise your

The only way you can encourage wanted behaviors in your Grey is through positive reinforcement. Offer lots of praise and attention when he does something you want him to.

bird lavishly in a high-pitched voice, offering a treat if you have one on hand or giving him a scratch on the head.

When your African Grey does something you don't want him to do, don't make a big scene about it. Making a scene over a bad behavior is positive reinforce-ment for your bird—he will not be able to tell the difference between how you react to his good behaviors and how you react to his bad behaviors. Birds love drama and will do anything to make you have a large reaction.

Training Don'ts

There are a few things you should never do to your African Grey during training (or any other time). These things will only result in breaking the trust that you and your African Grey should build in order to have a mutually satisfying relationship.

- Never hit, flick, squeeze, or throw your African Grey. This is animal abuse and will injure him, not to mention make him mistrust you.
- Never throw anything at your African Grey's cage to make him stop vocalizing. Throwing things at the cage will make your African Grey feel very insecure.
- Screaming at your African Grey will often cause him to scream louder or learn to mimic your screaming. If you scream, "Shut up!" your African Grey will learn this and say it at the most inopportune times!

- Never "play rough" with your African Grey. This will teach him to be aggressive and to bite.
- Never cover the cage for long periods during the day. If you have a sleeping infant or you simply need your bird to quiet down, you can cover the cage for an hour or so, but it's cruel to cover it for extended periods when your African Grey should be active.
- Never starve your African Grey as a training tool. Sure, your bird will be hungry and might do what you want him to do for a sunflower seed, but this might backfire on you and cause your bird to become ill.
- Never hold your African Grey's beak. This is akin to holding a person's hands behind his back. This will only frustrate your African Grey and he will come to mistrust you.
- Show no fear. Pulling your hand away from a bird that's bluffing a bite will teach him that he's powerful and that he can threaten you. Instead, use a stick or dowel to take the bird out of the cage—you should stick train your bird as soon as possible.

BASIC TRAINING LESSONS

African Greys are highly intelligent and can learn very complicated tricks and behaviors on command. However, training should start with the most simple, basic lessons first.

Teaching Your Bird to "Step Up"

Of all the behaviors you can teach your African Grey, the "step-up" command is possibly the most important. This lesson allows you to retrieve your African Grey at any time and is especially useful when he is being fussy or is in potential danger. "Step-up" is the act of your African Grey stepping gently onto your arm, hand, or finger without hesitation on command. An African Grey is not hatched knowing how to do this, so you must teach him. Perhaps your African Grey came to you already tame and hand trained—that's great! But it's still important to reinforce the step-up command so that it becomes second nature to you and to your Grey.

Assuming that you are teaching a tame or semi-tame Grey the step-up command, begin by allowing the bird to come out of his cage on his own. You win nothing by fishing him out violently and

The "step-up" command is the most important command to teach your African Grey and will be the foundation for other commands and tricks you teach him.

will only succeed in beginning your training session on a bad note. Place a perch on top of his cage, or let the bird climb onto a standing perch where he will be standing on a round dowel, not a flat surface. If your African Grey is a youngster, you can gently lift him out of the cage, but since he doesn't yet know how to step up, be careful not to pull too hard on his feet—he will grip the perch, not understanding what you want.

Once the bird is out, give him a treat, either a bit of yummy food or a good head scratching. This will show the bird that training sessions can be fun, and he will look forward to them. Next, begin rubbing your bird's chest and belly very softly and gently with the length of your index finger or your hand while talking to him, slowly increasing the pressure with which you push on his chest. You may have to repeat this for a few days, depending on the tameness of your Grey. Your semi-tame African Grey may not be sure what you are up to and might be wary of this kind of attention. Take things slowly and work to gain his trust. A tamer African Grey will often sit quietly, enjoying the attention.

Once you feel that your Grey is calm and used to this process, you can increase the pressure you place on his chest. Pushing slightly on an African Grey's chest will throw him slightly off balance, and he will lift up a foot to right himself. Place your finger or hand under the foot and lift the bird, if he allows it. If not, simply allow his foot to remain on your hand until the bird removes it. As you do this, tell your bird clearly to "step-up." You must always say "step-up" when he steps on to your hand—

Most Greys will learn the "step-up" command in one or two short sessions.

it is key that your African Grey associates the action of stepping onto your hand with the phrase.

Once your Grey is fairly good at stepping up, you can have him step from hand to hand, repeating the phrase "step up" and praising him. Your bird may hesitate at first, but soon he will know exactly what you want. Be sure that your training sessions last only a few minutes each, and try not to become frustrated if your Grey doesn't do exactly what you want right away. Ideally, training sessions should be short, perhaps 10 to 15 minutes twice a day, and should be incorporated into playtime. Remember, all training should be extremely pleasurable for a bird, or he will not learn a thing. Remember, too, that your hand or arm should be a firm, solid place for the bird to stand. If you're scared and you drop the bird or your arm is too wiggly, your Grey will be afraid to step up.

Most Greys will learn to step up easily in one or two short sessions—the more your African Grey trusts you, the easier he will be to teach him anything. Patience is key. Even if this command is the only behavior you teach your African Grey, is it by far the most valuable. If you make sure to say, "Step up" every time you lift your Grey, you will reinforce this important training every day and make life much easier for both of you.

The Whittle-Down Method

Fear of your African Grey's beak is an understandable, especially when the bird is untamed and behaving quite wildly. If this is the case, try the "whittle down" method. Begin by stick training your bird with the step-up command using a 3-foot dowel—use a width sized appropriately for a Grey.

Once your bird learns to step on to the stick and does it with ease, begin cutting the stick down, a few inches each week, until the stick is very short. Eventually, if you've done this slowly enough and have worked to gain your bird's trust, the stick will be so short that your African Grey will step onto your hand.

Stick Training

Stick training is simply teaching the "step-up" command using a perch or dowel instead of your finger. It is very important that your African Grey knows how to step onto a stick. The day may come when your Grey refuses to come down from the curtain rod or escapes from the house and is sitting high in a tree. An African Grey that has been stick trained will be easy to retrieve with a long dowel or broomstick. On the other hand, an African Grey that is not used to stepping on a stick will be terrified of it and you may lose the opportunity to save your bird from harm.

Teach "step-up" with a stick the same way you teach it with your finger. If your bird is terrified of the stick, you can leave the stick close to the cage where he will have a chance to view it and get used to its presence. You can even place the stick in your African Grey's cage so that the bird can chew it and stand on it. Use different sticks during training so that your bird learns not to be afraid of dowels and perches of any size.

ADVANCED TRAINING LESSONS

Once your African Grey has mastered the basic training lessons, he can now move onto more complicated lessons, such as trick training, learning to talk, and housetraining.

Trick Training

The first thing you need for trick training is a willing African Grey. You should have a good, trusting relationship with your bird, one that allows a lot of contact. Second, you need a quiet place where there is little to distract your bird from the task at hand.

Some of the easiest tricks capitalize on your bird's natural behaviors or behaviors that he already knows. For example, you can teach your bird to wave by using the "step-up" command. Once your bird has learned this command, offer your finger as if you want the bird to step up, say, "Wave hello!" (or "Wave goodbye"), then pull your hand away while the foot is in midair and say, "Good wave!" in your best, high-pitched praise voice. Wave your own hand at the bird, as if you are saying hello or goodbye. Repeat until your bird learns that this is a different command than step up and completes the wave successfully.

You can buy certain trick props, such as rollerskates or a basketball hoop, and train your bird to learn to use these items. These items tend to be pricey, but if you feel that your bird is willing to learn (perhaps he's taken to other tricks easily) you can try them. Don't be disappointed, however, if your African Grey doesn't take to tricks; some birds are more stubborn or are easily distracted, though most are intelligent enough to learn.

Once your Grey has mastered the basic training lessons, he can move on to more advanced trick training using props, such as hoops.

Teaching Your African Grey to Talk

Most, if not all, African Greys will learn various words and phrases. Even untamed African Greys will learn to mimic human speech. The key to teaching your African Grey to speak is repetition. The more you say something, the more likely your bird will pick it up. Speak clearly and don't tire of the repetition; eventually, your African Grey will catch on. Most African Greys will say their first words at one year of age or more, though some may speak sooner or later than that. Greys are known to be able to pick up a word after having heard it only one time. Be careful when using profanity around your bird, or you may have a foul-mouthed fowl on your hands!

Does your bird know what he is saying when it speaks? Evidence shows that Greys can be taught to understand and recognize number systems, shapes, colors, and other objects in the world and truly use these items in context. Your bird will only really understand what you are saying (and what he is saying) if you teach him to do so.

For example, if every time you give your bird water you say "water," your bird may come to associate the word "water" with the object "water" and begin to identify it in places other than in his dish, such as when the water is coming out of the kitchen faucet. Don't underestimate your bird's intelligence—he just might know more than you think!

Housetraining

Yes, African Greys actually can be housetrained. Birds don't have the ability to "hold it" the way humans do—a bird must be light in order to fly, so nature designed them such that any added weight is released quickly. There will be accidents—and that's okay—but housetraining your African Grey probably won't be difficult. Praise your bird for a job well done, and ignore (and clean up!) the unwanted "behavior."

Begin housetraining by recognizing the signs displayed just before your bird does his business. Usually, a bird will back up or squat a bit, lift the tail, and then eliminate. Each time your bird does his business, say, "Go poop" or some other phrase that will be his command. Your bird will come to associate the act of eliminating with the command.

After a few days of this, pick the bird up the moment your recognize the signs. Then place him in the desired place for his business and tell him to "Go poop." If your bird does well, praise him lavishly.

Another option is to place something under your bird—a paper plate or a sheet of newspaper—and ask him to "Go poop" onto the item. The bird will eventually learn that he must eliminate where or when you want him to.

There is a danger, however, in enforcing this command too strictly. For example, if a parrot is trained to only do his business in a certain location and you board him or change his location, he may not know to go there and will hold his wastes in. This may cause him to become ill, or at the very least, quite stressed. Therefore, it is best to only use this command occasionally.

ENTERTAINING YOUR AFRICAN GREY

Television

If you are going to be gone for an extended period of time during the day, you can leave the television or the radio on for your Grey, but choose a channel or a station that is going to be pleasant to listen to and not too distracting or grating. You don't want the noise or music to stress your bird, so leave the volume low, nor do you want your bird to pick up foul language or obnoxious noises, so an educational channel is a good choice.

The Great Outdoors

Taking your Grey outdoors for a change of scenery is fun and stimulating for your bird, but it can be risky. Make sure that you

Taking your Grey outdoors can be a great change of scenery for your bird, but make sure his wings are clipped and you carefully supervise his activity.

keep a close eye on your Grey at all times and that he is well clipped so that he can't fly away. In addition, don't take your Grey outdoors if there are predators around or if the weather is windy or cold. If the weather is hot, make sure to carry a spray bottle full of cool water and watch that your bird does not become overheated.

Traveling With Your African Grey

Many African Grey owners enjoy bringing their birds with them while traveling. Keeping your bird safe while traveling is easy when you have the right equipment and you plan ahead. First, your bird must have a safe carrier. It's dangerous to transport your African Grey in his home cage—toys and other swinging objects can injure your bird, and the multiple doors make it far easier to escape from than a carrier. Bird-specific carriers have a grating and door on the top so that the bird can see up instead of just out of one door—the door on top also makes it easier to catch a reluctant bird. Most airlines will accept a bird and will allow you to keep him under your seat, though you may have to pay an additional charge for the luxury.

Never leave your bird unattended in a car, or you might find him gone when you return—thieves love to steal birds because they know that birds are valuable. Always take your bird's first-aid kit in the case of an emergency, and find an avian veterinarian located at your destination spot before you leave.

Toys

Store-bought toys are nice for the Grey, as he will appreciate all of the interesting shapes and materials. You also can make your own interactive toys that will cost you nearly nothing and will provide hours of entertainment for your bird. The following are some simple toys you can make from things you probably already have in the home or can buy cheaply from a hardware store or craft store.

- Take one sheet of white tissue paper and place treats (nuts, millet spray, etc.) on one end and roll the treats up in the paper. Tie at both ends with sisal rope (the brown twine used to bundle packages) and place in your bird's cage or play gym. You can experiment with the shapes and sizes of the bundles.
- Place a clean, whole toilet paper roll in the cage and watch your Grey spend hours tearing at it.
- Collect paper towel rolls and cut them into 1-inch rings. String these on sisal rope and hang in cage—allow your bird to use these only with supervision in case he becomes tangled. You can experiment with all kinds of toys using these rings.
- Place non-toxic masking tape over one end of an empty toilet paper roll and put treats inside, then cap the other end with the tape and place in your bird's cage. You may have to rattle the toy so he knows that there's something inside. You can poke holes in it and hang it in the cage with sisal rope, but be sure to

Store-bought toys are great for Greys, as they will appreciate the interesting shapes, colors, and materials, but you can also create homemade toys for your Grey.

supervise the bird with this toy if you do so, especially because the tape can become stuck to the bird's beak!

- Cut newspaper into long, 1-inch strips, fold in half, then bundle it with sisal rope. The idea is for this to come out looking somewhat like a cheerleader's pompom. Tie it to the side of your bird's cage.

- Create all kinds of fun shapes using frozen treat sticks and non-toxic white glue. You can dye the sticks using vegetable dyes or by boiling them with beets.

- Your Grey will appreciate chewing safe, non-toxic green wood, especially if it comes with leaves and stems. Find branches from safe trees and make absolutely sure they haven't been sprayed with fungicide or pesticide. Wash all branches before you give them to your bird.

- Spoons and other safe, shiny objects are fun for your Grey to play with. Make sure the metal is non-toxic and has no sharp points. Toothbrushes are also fun, but make sure the bristles aren't attached with metal. You can put peanut butter on the toothbrush as an added treat. (Some people recommend against peanuts and peanut butter, so use sparingly or replace with almonds and almond butter.)

Educating African Grey Parrots

There's a difference between training a Grey and actually educating him. Training a Grey means that you ask him to do certain things and he does them. He may not really know why he's doing the behaviors but realizes that the behaviors bring him some kind of reward, usually attention and affection.

However, according to current research, Greys can truly be educated, too. Research on African Greys show that this species does indeed have the mental capacity to be educated and these birds can, in fact, understand a great deal about their environments and use language to manipulate those environments, similar to the way humans do. This is a remarkable discovery, considering that birds were once thought of as "bird brains."

Dr. Irene Pepperberg's studies on Greys, particularly on a Grey named Alex, have shown that Alex has cognitive abilities equal to that of a four-year-old child, with the emotional capacity of a two to three-year-old, a volatile combination. Beyond the formal research, Alex says many words and phrases that help him to communicate in everyday life, such as asking for a type of food that he wants or indicating when he would like to stop working for the day. Alex even works as a tutor for a new addition to the research facility, a young Congo Grey. Pepperberg is reluctant to say that the birds are learning language the way we understand it, but she does say that the birds are definitely communicating.

Alex was purchased at a pet store. He is an ordinary bird, with the exception of his extraordinary education. If you take the time to educate your Grey in a similar manner, your bird may begin picking up words and phrases and use them in context too. Don't expect your Grey to be just like Alex, however. Alex has a team of researchers working with him. Even so, one devoted owner could probably accomplish a lot.

To educate Alex, researchers use what is known as the model/rival technique. This technique requires that the subject (your African Grey) be able to observe someone else trying, failing, and eventually learning a certain skill. It also requires that the subject compete with the other person learning the skill.

Research shows that African Greys are so intelligent, they can be truly educated to understand their actions, environments, and the meanings of words.

For this kind of training, you will need two people: yourself (the teacher), and another person (the pupil who will act as a model and a rival for your bird). Find a quiet room where there are no distractions for the bird. Place the bird on a stand where he will be comfortable and sit down with the other pupil in front of him, so that the bird can observe the lesson. Find an object that you would want your bird to learn, such as a red apple. Show the human pupil the red apple and say, "Apple." The pupil will purposefully mispronounce the word, at which time you will repeat it. After a few tries, the pupil will get the word right, and will receive the apple and take a bite.

Then, turn to your bird and do the same thing. Your bird might just sit there blankly staring at you. That's okay. He doesn't get the apple until he says apple. Turn back to the pupil and repeat the lesson. Your Grey will be so desperate for that apple (out of jealously, primarily), he will probably at least try to repeat the word.

You can use this method for many objects in your home, especially for things that are important for your Grey to know.

You can begin educating your Grey in this way after he has begun substantial talking, when you know he is able to repeat words and phrases. Using objects that you know your Grey will like, such as a favorite food or a shiny object, like a spoon, is a good way to get him to begin learning.

GROOMING Your African Grey

African Greys do much of their own grooming, including keeping all of their feathers tidy and in place. A healthy African Grey has a strict regime of cleanliness. He will frequently preen his feathers and make sure that no debris lodges on his feet or beak. Preening may look to you like your African Grey is "picking nits," but this is a very normal behavior for a healthy bird, one that you can encourage through regular bathing. Grooming a bird also includes clipping the flight feathers (should you choose to do so), keeping the toenails trimmed, and making sure that the beak is properly aligned.

ALL ABOUT FEATHERS

Feathers are like hair in mammals, except that their function is far more important. Feathers began on certain dinosaurs, the first "birds," millions of years ago. Feathers are a bird's sole source of protection from water and the cold.

Well-groomed feathers are better able to protect the bird against moisture and chilly weather. Birds typically have high body temperatures, and their feathers help to keep them warm. You may notice your African Grey puffing his feathers when the temperature drops or when he's not feeling very well. Feathers are also used to attract the opposite sex. It's no wonder that your African Grey spends so much time preening and making sure every feather is in the proper place.

Types of Feathers

There are several types of feathers that grow on your African Grey.

Contour Feathers

These are the feathers that outline an African Grey's body, including the flight feathers and the feathers covering the body (coverts).

Flight Feathers

The wing is comprised of 20 flight feathers, 10 primary flight feathers (the long feathers at the end of the wing) and 10 secondary flight feathers (closer to the body).

There are several types of feathers that grow on your African Grey. The tiny feathers around your Grey's beak, nares, and eyes are called the semiplume feathers.

Semiplume Feathers

These are the tiny feathers around your African Grey's beak, nares, and eyes.

Down Feathers

Down feathers make up the undercoat of fluffy feathers beneath the contour feathers. These help to insulate the African Grey and keep him warm.

Powder Down Feathers

These feathers are small and white and grow just beneath the down feathers. Your African Grey crumbles these feathers during grooming, causing a white dust to coat the other feathers. You may notice a white plume of dust emitting from your bird when he ruffles and shakes his feathers. This dust helps to keep the feathers clean, but it often triggers allergies in an owner with a sensitive respiratory system. Bathing your bird, regular cleaning, and using an air purifier near the cage will cut down on this dust.

WING CLIPPING

Clipping a bird's wings is the act of cutting the primary flight feathers (only the first half of the feather) so that the bird is unable to fly very high or very far. These are the only feathers that you should *ever* clip. While wing clipping is a common and accepted practice, there is some evidence that clipping a bird's wings does frustrate the bird and can create some health problems if the bird is not active enough.

Wild African Greys spend most of their day flying around, looking for food and a safe place to sleep. That's a lot of exercise. A clipped bird will usually sit around all day picking out of his food dish unless you give him something to do with his time. You should make an extra effort to offer activities to a clipped African Grey. Play gyms, lots of toys, safe branches to chew, and blocks of safe, soft wood are all fun activities that will get your African Grey moving.

To Clip or Not to Clip

If you feel guilty about having your bird's wings clipped, you're not alone. Many people feel that wing clipping is cruel or that it hurts the bird. Actually, wing clipping does not hurt the bird any more than a haircut would hurt a human being, but flying is essential for the psychological well-being of a bird. This is an animal that is meant to fly, and when that ability is taken away, it can result in neurotic behaviors, such as self-mutilation. The bird will feel vulnerable and have little self-direction. If you can make your home absolutely safe, and you're positive that he can't escape or injure himself in any fashion, let him fly under supervision—he has wings for a reason. However, if you are not certain about your bird's safety, it is best to keep him clipped.

Wing clipping is vital to your African Grey's safety. An African Grey is certainly a danger to himself if allowed free flight through the average household. A free flighted African Grey could very easily burn himself on a hot stove, drown in the toilet, break his neck flying headfirst into closed windows or shiny mirrors, or put himself at risk to other dangers. There is also a huge risk of the bird escaping if you leave your African Grey free flighted. By clipping his wings, you can protect him from these dangers. Wing clipping is also painless if done correctly, and the feathers will grow back, usually in about five months if the bird is healthy, perhaps even sooner.

If you decide to clip your African Grey's wings, you have

Wing clipping is painless and important for your Grey's safety, but you must provide him with extra stimulation and activity to compensate for his inability to fly.

to go the extra mile to provide the freedom and stimulation that he would otherwise get from flying. To avoid neurotic behavior in your clipped African Grey, give him as much attention as possible. Also make sure he has enough space and exercise, giving him a lot of free time out of the cage and housing him in a large, safe cage of a size of at least 20 by 50 inches. This will give an African Grey enough room to spread his wings. You may also want to consider an aviary or habitat where your birds can fly without risk—many bird owners use this option and their birds are healthy and happy as a result.

Another option is to clip your new bird for an initial period of time, say six months to a year, until you and your bird come to know each other very well. This initial unflighted period will allow your bird to become used to you, your home, your other pets, and other family members. You must come to know and trust your bird's habits before you make the decision to let his flight feathers grow out. Remember, the potential for tragedy is always there.

How to Clip Your African Grey's Wings

If you've chosen to clip your African Grey's wing feathers, you should find a professional in your area who will clip them first and

If you decide to clip your African Grey's wings, it is best to have a professional show you how to do it first, so you can learn to hold him correctly and make the clip properly.

show you how to do it yourself. Many owners are squeamish about clipping their own African Grey's wings and choose to have someone else do it for them all the time. If you have an avian veterinarian, he or she is the best person to clip your African Grey's wings, and this way you have advantage of a veterinarian handling your bird. Because wing trimming is a traumatic event for a Grey, he may become angry with the person who does the clipping. This is another reason to have a professional do it.

How to Hold Your Grey Properly for Clipping

In order to clip your African Grey's wings, you must first learn how to hold him properly. You can't grab a bird any way you want, spread out a wing, and clip away. This can be very dangerous and might lead to injury. An African Grey has fragile bones that can break if you're too rough or don't hold him properly. A bird has a different way of breathing than we do, and it's possible to prevent him from breathing by holding him around the chest area, even lightly. Again, it's best to have your veterinarian show you how to do this first.

First, grasp the bird around the neck and the back, leaving the chest free. Your thumb should be on one side of the bird's neck, bracing the bottom of his jaw, and your index finger should be placed on the other side, doing the same. This looks a lot like you're choking the bird, bit it is actually the safest way to restrain him. Your Grey may struggle, so you can place a washcloth over his feet so he can grasp onto him. A bird that tends to bite can be grasped like this using a towel so he can chew on it and not on your fingers.

Once you feel that you're holding your Grey in the proper fashion, have someone else gently extend his wing and clip the first four feathers (the long ones at the end of the wing) for a young bird and the first five or six for an older bird, beginning at the point where the primary feather coverts end—those are the feathers on the upper side of the wing that end at the midpoint of the primary flight feathers. With a pair of sharp scissors, clip each feather, one by one, making a clean snip. Clip both wings. Greys (especially youngsters) are notoriously clumsy and should not receive a severe clip—leave enough feathers for your bird to glide to the ground, not hit it with an ungraceful clunk, which can cause severe injury to the breastbone.

Don't clip your African Grey's wings until you've watched someone do it in person and have had them show you how to hold your bird properly and which feathers to clip. Don't take a pair of sharp scissors to your bird's wings unless you're sure of what you're doing. It is important to note that an African Grey needs a very conservative clip. Most birds will need to have the seven flight feathers clipped, but the Grey may only need four or five—he's a heavy bird that can injure himself if he comes crashing to the floor because the wing clip is too severe.

MOLTING

When birds molt, they shed their feathers and make way for new ones to grow. The old feathers may have become ragged and not useful for insulation or flying anymore. A molt can happen once or twice a year, depending on the amount of light and warmth your African Grey is exposed to.

It's important to remember that this is a very stressful time for a bird. Your African Grey may become ill-tempered and not want to be touched at certain times. The newly growing feathers can be uncomfortable or tender. You will notice "pins" beginning to poke out from between your African Grey's other feathers, called pinfeathers. The "pin" is a sheath of material made of keratin that protects the new feather until he is ready to emerge. Your African Grey will spend time removing these sheathes, but will not be able to remove the ones on his head. If your bird allows head scratching, you can gently remove them just as his mate would.

Pinfeathers and new feathers that have just emerged from the sheath have a blood supply and will bleed if injured or broken. This often happens with a wing feather, especially in a clipped bird lacking full-grown wing feathers that would protect a new feather from breaking. If you notice a bleeding feather, perhaps one that was clipped during wing trimming, don't panic. Pull the feather straight out from the root with one quick motion, and the bleeding will stop immediately. A pair of needle-nosed pliers is good for this purpose and should be kept in your bird's first-aid kit. If you're squeamish about this, apply styptic powder to the bleeding area and take your bird to your avian veterinarian as soon as possible.

Molting birds do not lose all of their feathers at once. Most molts are many weeks or months long, and feathers are replaced gradually. If you notice bald patches on your African Grey's body or his feathers become so thin you can see the skin beneath them, take your bird to your avian veterinarian right away—

Molting occurs when birds shed their feathers and make way for new ones to grow. The molting period can happen once or twice a year.

there may be a serious problem or your bird might be feather chewing or plucking.

Caring for the Molting African Grey

Because molting is such a stressful time for an African Grey, he will need special care to make this time more comfortable. Regular misting with warm water is helpful in softening the pinfeathers. Only mist your bird in temperate weather and when there's adequate time for him to dry before evening.

In addition, offer your African Grey an extra-nutritious diet while he's molting, including a protein source, such as hardboiled eggs or boiled chicken. You shouldn't notice any difference in the way your African Grey behaves, eats, plays, or responds to you during a molt, but there is the possibility he might behave differently while the new feathers are emerging. Your bird may not want to be touched as often and may even be reluctant to leave the cage. Respect his wishes during this stressful time.

Your African Grey's toenails should have a graceful, half-moon curve, like those on this Timneh African Grey.

TRIMMING THE TOENAILS

If you play with your African Grey regularly, you might notice that his toenails pinch and prick you uncomfortably and may even break your skin. This is the time to trim his toenails. If your African Grey has a conditioning perch made of concrete or another rough material, you may only have to trim the toenails three or four times a year.

Your African Grey's toenails should have a graceful half-moon curve to them; if they extend well beyond this, your bird might have a medical problem related to a nutritional deficiency or may not have adequate perches. See your veterinarian if your African Grey's toenails seem unusual in any way.

A bird's toenails are like our toenails—there's a dead part and a living part, called the quick. When trimming your bird's nails, you only want to cut off the dead part of the nail. Cutting into the quick is very painful and causes bleeding. To prevent this, you will want to trim the nails very conservatively, taking off the very tip of the nail. You can use a small human nail clipper to trim your bird's nails, which may be a two-person job—one to hold the bird properly and one to trim the nails. If bleeding does occur, simply apply styptic power to the wound, and it should stop.

Quickly clipping one toenail a day, while your Grey isn't suspecting it, is a great way to complete the job of clipping without causing your bird distress. It takes a few days this way, but you won't have to traumatize the bird by restraining him.

BATHING YOUR AFRICAN GREY

If you offer your African Grey water in a large coop cup, he may bathe himself, though most Greys are reluctant to get thoroughly wet. Some very tame African Greys may enjoy sitting on a special perch while their owner is showering. A mister simulating rain is a good way to get your African Grey to bathe as well. When the weather is warm and if your African Grey is well clipped, you can take him outdoors in a safe spot and bathe him with a light shower from your garden hose.

Bathing is important for your African Grey, not only because it keeps the bird clean, but also because it encourages preening. You bird only needs clean, fresh water for bathing—there are bathing products that you can buy from the pet shop, but they are not really necessary. Bathe your bird in warm weather and in the daytime only, allowing plenty of time for him to dry thoroughly. Never use soaps or other detergents—plain, fresh water will do.

THE FEATHER-PICKING GREY

Greys are high on the list of notorious feather chewers and pickers. This is because they are highly sensitive birds that need to have their energies directed to the proper places, such as chewing

If you provide your Grey with perches made of concrete or other rough materials, you may only have to clip his nails three or four times a year.

If you see your Grey picking at his feathers, immediately draw his attention to another activity.

on toys, shredding paper, and playing with an owner. If a Grey is neglected, unhappy in his circumstances, receives a fright, or experiences undesired change in his environment, he may begin to chew or pick his feathers.

Once this becomes a habit, it is very difficult to change and may go on for years, until much of the bird is bald. Balding birds eventually begin picking their skin, causing lesions and infections. To discourage your Grey from picking, provide him with a lot to do, and teach him how to play. Provide a lot of gentle, hands-on attention. If your bird begins to pick, take immediate action to transfer the behavior onto something else, like toilet paper tied to the cage bars, sisal and floss toys, strips of shredding fabric (use with supervision only in case the threads become wrapped around a leg or neck, or make sure the threads are short), bundled and tied strands of newspaper, and other items that will distract the bird from his own feathers and act out the over-preening behavior on something else.

You should make an appointment with your veterinarian the moment you detect picking. Often, picking is a sign of illness.

IS BEAK GROOMING NECESSARY?

There should never be a reason for you to groom your African Grey's beak. Eating hard items, chewing toys, and grooming his beak on a conditioning perch will all help to keep it trimmed and properly aligned. In some cases, when an African Grey is ill or has a severe nutritional deficiency, the beak may become elongated and may interfere with eating. This is a case for a veterinarian's treatment. You can severely injure your African Grey by trying to trim the beak yourself.

HEALTH CARE for Your African Grey

A well-cared-for African Grey can live to be more than 50 years old, but it's a sad fact that these birds rarely live beyond 10 to 15 years due to accident or illness, many of which can be easily prevented. This chapter will help you choose a veterinarian, recognize the signs of illness in your African Grey, explain how to create a safe household environment, and give you tips on how to deal with common emergencies.

CHOOSING AN AVIAN VETERINARIAN

An avian veterinarian is a doctor who has been trained to treat the illnesses and injuries of birds. The avian veterinarian has experience with recognizing and treating illnesses particular to birds, whose bodily systems are far different from those of a dog or cat. Your avian veterinarian is your first line of defense in keeping your African Grey healthy.

You can locate an avian veterinarian by calling the Association of Avian Veterinarians at (561) 393-8901 or going to their site on the Internet at www.aav.org. The American Federation of Aviculture also has information on how to find an avian veterinarian in your area. You can contact them by phone at (602) 484-0931 or on the Internet at www.afa.birds. You can also ask the person from whom you purchased the bird if he or she has any recommendations for a qualified avian veterinarian.

African Greys that are well cared for can live to be more than 50 years old, especially when given proper veterinary care, diet, and a safe environment.

Choosing an avian veterinarian takes a bit more effort than just finding one near you home. You will want to make sure that the doctor is open to your questions and concerns and experienced with birds. Ask the veterinarian if he or she has birds of his or her own—it's a good sign if this is the case. Find out what hours the office is open and what the emergency policy is. When you visit the office, look around to make sure that it's clean and talk to the staff members to see if they are friendly and efficient. Remember, this is a relationship that will last the lifetime of your bird, and you might as well make it a good one.

The "Well-Bird" Checkup

Once you acquire your new African Grey, you should make an appointment in the first three days to see an avian veterinarian near you. This "well-bird" checkup will ensure that your bird is healthy and it will begin a relationship with your avian veterinarian. Many veterinarians will not treat emergencies unless the patient is already registered at the office, so you might find yourself in a dire situation if you haven't created this valuable relationship.

Yearly Checkups

You should take your African Grey to the avian veterinarian at least once a year, around the same time. This will enable the doctor to weigh the bird and do some routine tests that will show any changes and indicate any potential disorders. This is also a good time to discuss your bird's diet and have the doctor trim his nails as well.

QUARANTINE

Quarantine is traditionally a period of 40 days in which a new bird is kept separate from birds already established in the household. Some people choose to shorten this period to 30 days and find no harm in doing so. If you have other birds, you should definitely quarantine your African Grey when you first bring him home.

During the period of quarantine, a new bird is watched for signs of illness. You should feed and water the new bird after you care for your other birds, change your clothing, and disinfect your hands after any contact with the bird or its cage. Quarantine is the only way to prevent a new bird from passing a potential illness to the birds you already own. It is sometimes not possible to completely

Your African Grey should see his avian veterinarian for a checkup at least once a year to assess his health and to ensure that he is not suffering from any illness.

separate a new bird from established birds, but you should try to do your best to keep contact at a minimum while the new bird is being quarantined.

SIGNS AND SYMPTOMS OF ILLNESS

Like most birds, African Greys tend to hide their illnesses until the effects are quite advanced. A wild African Grey that shows himself to be ill is vulnerable to predators and will try to behave as normally as possible for as long as possible. Your African Grey has the same instinct. Knowing what to look for in an ailing African Grey will help you to recognize the illness early, which is key to treatment and speedy recovery. If you see any of the following symptoms in your bird, call your veterinarian so he or she can decide on the course of action that is best for your bird.

Excessive Sleeping

An ill African Grey may sleep too much, especially during the day. Sleeping on the bottom of the cage with his feathers fluffed up is particularly significant.

If you notice that your African Grey has a fluffed appearance and is not molting, he may be ill.

Fluffed-Up Appearance

If you notice that your African Grey is fluffy, he may be trying to maintain his body temperature and could be fighting off an illness.

Loss of Appetite

You should know how much food and what types of food your African Grey is consuming each day. If you notice that your bird is not eating or is eating far less than usual, he could be ill.

Change in Attitude

If your African Grey seems listless and is not behaving in his usual manner (for example, if he has become cranky or limp), this could indicate a problem.

Lameness
If your African Grey can't use its feet or hold up his head, there's definitely something wrong. Possible reasons include injury and egg binding. Consult an avian veterinarian immediately.

Panting or Labored Breathing
These symptoms might signify a respiratory illness or overheating.

Discharge
If you notice runniness or discharge on the eyes, nares, or vent, there may be an illness present.

Change in Droppings
Your African Grey's droppings should consist of a solid-green portion, white urates (overlapping the green portion), and a clear liquid. If the droppings are discolored (very dark-green, black, yellow, or red) and there has been no change in diet (such as feeding beets or blueberries), there might be a problem. Also, if there's a pungent odor or the droppings seem far more liquid than usual, call your veterinarian immediately.

Debris Around the Face or on Feathers
This indicates poor grooming or regurgitation, both of which are potential signs of illness.

Seizures
If your African Grey is flailing in his cage and there are no obvious signs that he is caught in parts of its cage or a toy, place the bird in a safe carrier and rush him to your avian veterinarian.

Severe Change in Feather Quality or Quantity
If your African Grey begins to lose feathers in patches, or you notice him shredding them or picking them out, call your veterinarian for an appointment.

COMMON DISEASES AND AILMENTS
African Greys are prone to several diseases and ailments, many

of which are preventable and treatable by your avian veterinarian. The following section details a few of the most common ailments that African Greys are known to carry or contract. Use this information as a guide only—never try to diagnose or treat your African Grey without consulting your avian veterinarian first. There are treatments available over-the-counter, but many of these often make the situation worse for an ill bird. Never medicate or treat your bird for a suspected illness until you seek the advice of a professional.

Nutritional Disorders

An African Grey with a poor diet may soon begin to suffer from a variety of disorders, including obesity, tumors, foot problems, feather disorders, mouth lesions, and a weakened immune system that will leave the bird vulnerable to disease. Common symptoms of nutritional disorders include an overgrown beak, yeast infections, fatty tumors, lameness, swelling in the feet, and discoloration of the feathers in extreme cases.

To ensure that your African Grey does not suffer from these easily preventable ailments, offer a balanced diet and if necessary according to the advice of your avian veterinarian, include nutritional supplements in the recommended doses. Poor nutrition will cut your African Grey's lifespan by more than half of its potential years.

To ensure that your Grey does not suffer from easily preventable nutritional disorders, provide him with a healthy, balanced diet every day.

Hypocalcemia

Greys suffer from hypocalcemia (low calcium in the blood) more frequently than other companion birds. Hypocalcemia can cause seizures and bone fractures. Make sure to feed a diet rich in calcium, preferably from natural sources. Have your veterinarian check your bird's blood calcium level and give a calcium injection if it is low.

Parasites

Giardia

Giardia is a one-celled protozoan that can affect your African Grey, as well as other animals in the house and even you. Giardia is passed through tainted food or water and distresses the digestive tract. It can cause diarrhea, itching, the inability to digest foods, and weight loss, among other symptoms. Have your veterinarian test your bird for this problematic parasite that is often resistant to treatment.

Worms

Worms are sometimes found in the digestive tract of companion birds and should be tested for on your first veterinary visit. If worms are found, routine tests and treatments should be performed on the bird—getting rid of these pesky worms can take quite some time.

Feather Mites

The feather mite is not very common in African Greys but can plague birds that live outdoors in filthy conditions. Red mites feed on their host's blood and are highly contagious, though not frequently seen in African Greys. If you suspect mites, do not attempt to treat them yourself—see your avian veterinarian for treatment options.

Bacterial Infections

Mycobacterium avium

Mycobacterium avium is responsible for the tuberculosis infection in African Greys and can be transmitted in food, water, or by unclean cage conditions. Avian tuberculosis can be transmitted to humans with compromised immune systems, so the caretaker must be careful to avoid infection. This disease is principally a digestive infirmity in birds. Symptoms include weight loss and digestive disorders.

Psittacosis/Parrot Fever

Psittacosis, also called chlamydiosis and Parrot Fever, is also transmittable to humans and causes respiratory distress symptoms in both humans and birds. Psittacosis is transmitted through droppings and other contaminated discharge. It is not very common these days, but it does still occur.

Viral Infections

PBFD

Psittacine Beak and Feather Disease (PBFD) is an incurable, highly contagious disease that includes feather loss and beak lesions. Diagnosis is through a blood test, and euthanasia is normally suggested if a bird tests positive. This disease is fatal. Symptoms include feather loss, abnormal feather growth, and a generally ill condition.

Polyoma Virus

Polyoma virus typically affects young birds, though adult birds carry the disease and transmit it to their young; they, in turn, die around the time of fledging. Polyoma virus occurs mainly among breeding birds, though households with many birds are susceptible as well, especially if you are going to be bringing young birds into the household. There is no treatment for polyoma virus at the moment, though there is a vaccine. Have your avian veterinarian test your bird for this disease.

Pacheco's Disease

Pacheco's disease is a type of viral hepatitis that affects the liver. It is fatal and is primarily diagnosed upon death, which occurs quickly. Pacheco's is a highly contagious disease and can be transmitted easily when acquiring a new bird, which is why it is important to enforce strict quarantine at all times.

Fungal Infections

Candidiasis

Yeast infections, or *candidiasis*, affect the mouth and digestive system and can involve the respiratory system as well. Your African

Grey generally has a certain amount of yeast in its system, but when it is undernourished or has been through a regime of antibiotics, the fungus yeast can grow to excess, causing health problems.

An African Grey with a yeast infection will have a sticky material in its mouth and may have white mouth lesions. Regurgitation and digestive problems may occur as well. Treatment by a veterinarian is required. Even though this condition is not immediately serious, if left untreated, it can cause death.

Offering your African Grey foods rich in vitamin A, such as green leafy vegetables and orange fruits and vegetables, can help prevent yeast infections. Vitamin A supplements also may be recommended.

Aspergillosis

Aspergillosis is a fungal infection that causes respiratory distress and can be deadly for an African Grey. Any changes in your African Grey's breathing and vocalization or gasping and wheezing can signify this infection. Aspergillosis is difficult to treat and may take months of medication and treatment. You can prevent this infection by keeping your African Grey's housing and surroundings very clean, dry, and free of mold and mildew.

The average home can be dangerous to the curious African Grey, so you must take steps to "African Grey proof" your home to protect your bird from these dangers.

Keeping Your Home Safe for Your African Grey

Though many African Greys can live a long time and can even outlive their owners, some of these healthy birds do not make it to a ripe old age due to accidents in the home. The average family home is extremely dangerous for the curious African Grey, as he will manage to find his way into things you never imagined, often with serious consequences. The following section describes the most common household dangers to the African Grey and what you can do to "African Grey-proof" your home in order to protect your pet from these dangers.

Other Pets

The family dog poses a huge threat to the African Grey, and the family cat is an even deadlier enemy. Certain breeds of dog, such as terriers and sighthounds, are particularly dangerous to have around a bird—their instincts tell them to pounce on small, quick-moving objects. One slight nip from a dog, even in play, can mean death for your African Grey. Even if your dog is smaller than your African Grey, you don't want to take the chance of the dog and the bird getting into a fight.

While dogs of certain breeds may be able to be trained not to go near a bird, a cat should never be trusted, not for a moment. Cats don't even have to bite to kill a bird—they have types of bacteria on their claws and in their mouths that are extremely toxic to birds. This means that one scratch can cause an African Grey to die within 48 hours unless immediate treatment by a veterinarian is sought. Supervise all of your animals when they are in the room together.

Standing Water

Standing water is a strong temptation for an African Grey, because he may want to take a drink. Unfortunately, the bird may fall into a pool that is too deep for his size, and he may find himself unable to get out.

Many African Greys drown in toilets, large dog bowls, fish tanks, fish bowls, ponds, fountains, Jacuzzis, full sinks (with dishes soaking), and pots of boiling water—this last instance is especially awful. Keep your toilet lids down at all times and keep all exposed water covered, even if you think your African Grey can't get to it.

Nonstick Cookware and Appliances

Any cookware labeled "nonstick" emits an odorless fume that, when heated, can kill a bird within a matter of moments. It was previously thought that the fumes only occurred when the nonstick surface was overheated, but research now indicates that they are emitted at even low levels of heat.

Many items other than pots and pans can have nonstick surfaces. These include heat lamps, portable heaters, plates on irons, ironing board covers, stovetop burners, drip pans for burners, broiler pans, griddles, cooking utensils, woks, waffle makers, electric skillets, deep fryers, crock pots, popcorn poppers, coffeemakers, breadmakers, nonstick rolling pins, lollipop molds, stockpots, roasters, pizza pans, and curling irons. Even a well-ventilated room isn't safe when there are nonstick items being used. Toss your nonstick items and get used to cleaning pots and pans with a heavy-duty scrubber! Do not chance killing your bird for convenient cooking.

If you notice that your African Grey is in distress and there's no apparent reason, check for gas leaks or other fume-causing agents, such as scented candles, fireplaces, and heated nonstick surfaces.

Common Household Products

Keep all household cleaning items away from your African Grey. These include soaps, drain cleaners, laundry detergents, floor cleanser, and bathroom cleaners, all of which might be a tempting treat for your African Grey but will carry tragic consequences.

Items commonly kept in a garage should be stored neatly away from your bird. These include fertilizers, pesticides, and barbeque products, such as charcoal and lighter fluid. Realize that your African Grey can easily tear through paper bags.

Items that are regularly sprayed into the air can cause severe respiratory distress or death. These include air fresheners, fabric fresheners, and even scented candles. African Greys will want to munch on candle beads or other waxy items, like crayons. Markers, pencils, and pens can also be deadly.

Toxic Houseplants

African Greys are chronic nibblers, always tearing something to bits the moment you turn your back. Your houseplants are a serious temptation for your African Grey, as he is naturally attracted to

African Greys often sample houseplants, so make sure the plants you keep in your home are not toxic to Greys, and try to keep them out of your bird's reach.

them. Even one nibble of a toxic plant can be poisonous for your bird and can cause death. See the Appendix for a list of plants that are both toxic and non-toxic to your bird.

Ceiling Fans

Birds have a natural instinct to climb or fly to the highest spot that they can find. A high spot is generally safe from predators and is a good lookout point. A ceiling fan seems like the perfect spot for a fully-flighted African Grey. However, one hit from the blade of a ceiling fan is all it takes to bring your African Grey down for good. Make sure all ceiling fans are kept off or have them removed.

Open Windows and Doors

The threat of a fully-flighted African Grey winging out of an open door or window is a serious one—many African Greys that take flight outdoors are never seen again. Keep all doors and windows securely closed or screened when your African Grey is out of its cage, or make sure that its wings are clipped properly. Even if you believe that your bird is attached to you and would never leave, a loud noise such as a car backfiring might frighten your African Grey into flight, and he may become confused and not find his way back.

Having your bird fly away is a heartbreaking experience. If your bird flies away, there's still hope that the two of you will be reunited—your bird is not necessarily gone for good. First, follow him with your eyes and watch where he goes—this is a crucial time. If you bird is very friendly, you may be able to coax it down from a tree or other spot with a treat, such as a peanut. Keeping an eye on your bird until nightfall is the key to a quick recovery. Once it gets dark, your bird will "roost," and you might be able to capture him easily with a bird net.

If your bird lives in a pair or has other bird pals in the house, take the other birds outside in a safe carrier and encourage them to whistle or talk to the lost bird. Take your bird's cage outside, fill it with treats, and leave the door open—he might come down at the sight of its cage filled with treats. It's a good idea to make a recording of your bird's vocalizations—the sound of his own voice may bring your African Grey back home. A Grey might also come down at the sight of his owner lavishing affection onto another pet or another person.

If you are unable to pinpoint the location of your lost bird right away, begin making calls to all of your local pet shops, veterinary offices, and shelters; describe your bird and offer a reward for his safe return. Make fliers and posters and hang them in places that get a lot of foot traffic, such as grocery stores. If you don't have a photo of your bird, clip one out of a book or magazine.

Most foods that humans eat are acceptable for African Greys, too, but never feed your bird avocado, rhubarb, chocolate, alcohol, caffeine, or raw onion.

Human Feet and Doorjambs

African Greys that are allowed to walk around on the floor are in danger of being stepped on or crushed in a doorjamb. Try not to allow your African Grey access to the floor, especially if your carpeting is gray!

Toxic Foods

Most foods are perfectly fine for an African Grey to ingest, with the exception of avocado (parts of it are toxic), rhubarb, chocolate, alcohol, caffeine, and raw onion. These items can make an African Grey very ill, or even kill him. Junk foods, such as salty snacks or sweet deserts, are not toxic, but they're not great for your African Grey, either.

Electrical Devices and Wires

Keep all wires wrapped and hidden away from your bird. Lamps and other plugged-in appliances do not make good play gyms.

Heavy Metals

Keep your African Grey away from stained glass decorations, costume jewelry, lead fishing weights, or other materials containing metals that can be toxic to your African Grey. The material with which many people use to build cages is often dipped in zinc to prevent rusting. Because this zinc is deadly for your African Grey, you must rinse and scrub all homemade cage material thoroughly before housing birds.

Temperature Fluctuations

African Greys are sensitive to extreme heat and extreme cold. They can die from overheating and are prone to frostbite in cold, windy conditions. If you live in an extreme climate, be sensitive to your African Grey's temperature requirements.

Mirrors and Glass

An African Grey that has full flight will not know the difference between empty space and a clean window or mirror. In your African Grey's eyes, it seems as if he could fly right through these solid objects, but this mistake carries drastic consequences. Many birds break their necks this way. This is a great excuse to leave your windows dirty, or you should at least to buy pretty decals to put on them.

Human Medicines

Never try to treat your bird with human medicines, as these remedies may react very differently in your bird's delicate system than they do in yours. Treat your bird only with medicines that your avian veterinarian has provided and prescribed.

Emergency Response Tips

Sometimes it's not easy to get to an avian veterinarian right away when an emergency occurs, so you will have to comfort and treat your African Grey on your own until you can get to the doctor's office. The following section lists tips for dealing with common emergencies.

Creating a Hospital Cage

A hospital cage is important to have on hand for many emergencies and illnesses. It's a comfortable, warm, safe place for your African Grey to calm down and recuperate from a trauma or sickness. Simply line an aquarium with paper towels and place a heating pad on low to medium underneath one half of the aquarium—your bird must be able to move away from the heat if it gets too warm.

Cover the aquarium with a mesh aquarium cover and drape a towel over ³/₄ of the tank. Place a very shallow dish of water (a weak bird can drown in even an inch of water) in the cage, as well as some treats, millet spray, and seeds or pellets. Do not include toys or perches, but you can include a rolled-up hand towel for snuggling. Place the cage in a quiet location and clean the papers when they become soiled.

You can also make your bird's own cage into a hospital cage by covering ³/₄ of the cage with a heavy blanket and aiming a heat lamp near your African Grey's favorite perch. Be careful, however, that the heat lamp does not have a nonstick coating, which can emit potentially deadly fumes. Carefully read the information that comes with the lamp.

Contact with Poison

If your bird comes in contact with poison and you notice evidence of vomiting; paralysis; bleeding from the eyes, nares, mouth, or vent; seizures; or shock, and you're not able to get to an avian veterinarian right away, call the National Animal Poison Control Center 24-hour Poison Hotline at (800) 548-2423, (888)

4-ANIHELP or (900) 680-0000 and ask for help. You will need to have an idea of the poison your bird has ingested, and there may be a small fee for the services.

Dealing With Broken Blood Feathers

Sometimes a wing or tail feather will break in the middle of the growth process and begin to bleed. This is a very typical occurrence with Greys and is not a serious injury; in fact, it's one you can deal with yourself. Keep a styptic powder or pencil on hand in the case of a bleeding emergency such as this one, and apply the product until the bleeding has stopped.

Next, if the feather is large (wing or tail) you will need to remove it with a pair of needle-nosed pliers. While restraining the bird (you may need two people for this procedure), simply grasp the broken feather with the pliers close to the shaft of the feather, hold the bird firmly, and pull it straight out. This will stop the bleeding and prevent infection.

If you are too squeamish to do this yourself, or if you would like to see this procedure done before you do it yourself (always a good idea), take your African Grey to your avian veterinarian.

Oil on the Feathers

If your African Grey becomes soaked in oil, he will no longer be able to regulate his body temperature, a condition that can be deadly. Dust the oil-soaked bird with cornstarch or flour; then gently bathe him in a small tub of warm water and some mild, grease-fighting dish soap. Don't scrub the bird. You may have to repeat this process several times. Keep the bird in a warm hospital cage until most of the oil is removed and he is dry.

Immediate Response to Overheating

An overheated African Grey will pant and spread his wings in an attempt to cool himself. If this is unsuccessful and the heat does not abate, the bird may lose consciousness and even die. If you notice that your African Grey is becoming overheated, remove him immediately to a cooler place and run a fan near his cage. Lightly mist the bird with cool water and offer drops of cool water in his mouth. Never set an African Grey out in the sun unless he has a shady spot to retreat to, and never leave any bird in a closed car on a warm day—birds are easily overcome by heat.

Response to Egg Binding

Occasionally, a female African Grey, even one housed alone and without a mate, will become calcium deficient or have a disorder of the reproductive tract, and an egg will become stuck inside her. This can cause paralysis and even death if left untreated. If you notice your female bird lying on the bottom of the cage with her feathers fluffed, if you see her panting, or if she has a distended belly and her droppings are large and watery, she may be trying to lay an egg.

Give her some time to lay it on her own, but if 24 hours pass and she hasn't laid it, you may need to intervene. If you can't get her to an avian veterinarian right away, place a few drops of mineral oil or olive oil in her vent (just at the outside of it) and a couple of drops in her mouth. This may help to lubricate the area and ease the egg out. If this doesn't work, try it again, move her into a very warm hospital cage, and call your avian veterinarian. Even if she passes the egg, she might need an examination so that the situation doesn't occur again.

YOUR AFRICAN GREY'S FIRST-AID KIT

Here is a list of essential items for a bird first-aid kit. Keep these items in a small tackle box for convenient access when you need them.

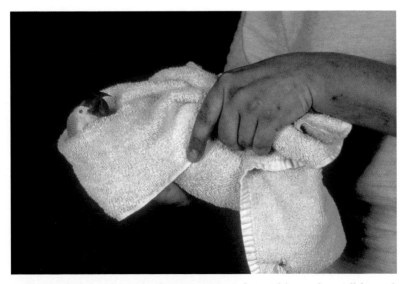

It is a good idea to keep towels in your Grey's first-aid kit so they will be easily accessible should you need them to hold your bird during an emergency.

- Antibiotic ointment (for small wounds, use a non-greasy product only—oil prevents a bird from keeping in body heat)
- Alcohol (for sterilizing tools)
- Baby bird formula (can be used for adults having a difficult time eating)
- Bandages and gauze
- Bottled water (you may need clean, fresh water to flush out a wound or clean your bird of debris)
- Cotton balls
- Cotton swabs
- Dishwashing detergent (mild, for cleaning oil off of feathers)
- Electrolyte solution, for human babies (for reviving a weak bird)
- Eyewash
- Heating pad (always allow your bird the option of moving off of the heating pad)
- Hydrogen Peroxide (always use in a weak solution with water)
- Nail clippers
- Nail file
- Needle-nosed pliers (for broken blood feathers)
- Non-greasy first aid lotion
- Penlight
- Saline solution
- Sanitary wipes
- Sealed bag or can of your bird's base diet (in case of evacuation)
- Sharp scissors
- Small, clean towels (for holding or swabbing)
- Small transport cage
- Spray bottle (for misting)
- Styptic powder (to stop bleeding)
- Syringe (without needle)
- Tweezers
- Veterinarian's phone number

QUESTIONS Frequently Asked on African Grey Care

The following chapter is composed of common questions African Grey owners have about their birds and their care. The answers to these frequently asked questions should serve as a handy reference to any African Grey owner.

Q: *Should I buy a Timneh or a Congo Grey?*

A: That depends largely on your budget and your family situation. Both birds make excellent pets—both are intelligent and can learn complex behaviors. They are also both proficient talkers. However, the Timneh is less expensive than the Congo and tends to be a better family bird, able to accept many people as part of the flock, and he is more apt to accept changes in the home.

Q: *Should I buy more than one African Grey?*

A: Well, that depends. These birds are quite a handful, and you might not even be able to handle one Grey, let alone two. The average household has room for only one African Grey. These birds are quite demanding of their owner's attention. If you are home all day, are extremely dedicated to your animals, and are very experienced with birds, two or more African Greys might be fine for you. However, realize that the more birds you have, the less individual attention each one will get. The Grey thrives on a lot of attention and can become extremely unhappy when he perceives that he's being neglected.

African Greys require a lot of time and attention, but if you are extremely dedicated to your animals and have experience with birds, owning two or more African Greys is acceptable.

Q: *How do I know if my African Grey was smuggled?*

A: There are a few ways of telling whether the African Grey you are interested in buying was smuggled or not. First, look at the band on the bird's foot. If it is a closed band that looks like a ring with no gaps in it, the bird was domestically bred, not smuggled. If the band is open (obviously tightened on with a tool), the bird was probably caught in the wild and brought into this country before 1991, when most exotic bird importation ceased.

If the bird does not have a band on his leg, you can tell if he is a baby by looking at his eyes: the juveniles will have darker, softer eyes, and the adults have yellow eyes with black pupils. If the bird is very young, he was probably captive bred, especially if you are buying him from a breeder and are allowed to see the parent birds.

Always buy your birds from a reputable source, such as an established breeder or reputable pet shop that has documentation about your bird. Never buy a bird from the back of a truck or buy a bird for a price well below the market standard—these birds may have been smuggled or stolen. At the very least, you will not get a health guarantee, nor your money back should the bird become ill soon after you acquire him. Buyer, beware.

Q: *Is my African Grey male or female?*

A: African Greys are monomorphic, meaning that there is no visible difference between the males and the females. You can have your bird sexed by your avian veterinarian, or you can send a feather or a blood sample to a company for DNA testing. However, there is no difference in pet quality between the sexes, so there is no real pressing need to find out your bird's sex.

Q: *Do male or female African Greys make better pets?*

A: The difference in pet quality between the sexes is negligible. Don't worry about the sex of your bird unless you eventually want to breed it.

Q: *Does my African Grey need grit?*

A: No, certainly not. In fact, if an African Grey eats too much grit, it can become impacted in the crop, causing severe malnutrition and even death. Do not feed any parrot grit.

Q: *Will my African Grey talk?*

A: Probably. Most African Greys can learn to talk. Simply repeat words and phrases that you want your African Grey to learn. Some individuals talk better than others, but it is the rare African Grey that will not learn at least a few words. It's best if the words and phrases you repeat mean something to you. Words said in earnest are picked up more easily than robotic repetition.

Don't stress out if your bird is over a year old and hasn't yet learned a few words. Your bird isn't dumb—he may be responding to other stimuli that are preventing him from talking. For example, if you have several birds, your African Grey may enjoy "talking" to them in his own bird language, rather than learning your language. If you whistle a lot around your

Males and females make equally good pets, so you will not need to distinguish the sex of your African Grey unless you plan to breed it.

African Grey, you may notice that he picks up the whistles easily but still doesn't talk—birds that learn to whistle well before they learn to talk may not talk as soon as birds that aren't exposed to much whistling. This is not always the case, of course, but it's something to think about.

Q: *Should I take my African Grey to the veterinarian?*

A: Absolutely. It is very important to take your new African Grey to the avian veterinarian for a well-bird checkup. This way the veterinary office has a record of your bird's health. Also, many veterinarians will not take an emergency unless the bird is already a patient. Your bird should visit the veterinarian at least once a year, even if he is healthy. Of course, if you notice the slightest symptom of illness, you should take your bird to the doctor immediately.

Q: *My African Grey seems ill—what should I do?*

A: First, call your avian veterinarian and describe the symptoms your bird is having. If you can schedule a walk-in appointment, do so. If the illness strikes in the middle of the night and you can't reach your veterinarian, place your bird in a hospital cage and make sure there's a heat source (heat lamp or heating pad) that warms your bird.

Q: *Should I clip my African Grey's wings?*

A: Wing clipping is a personal choice, though the fact remians that most African Greys that live in the typical home setting live longer and aren't prone to flying away when they are clipped. However, birds are meant to fly—flying offers a bird a wonderful form of exercise and is essential to his psychological health. Building habitats and aviaries for African Greys so that they can fly free in a safe space is an excellent solution.

Q: *Should I breed my African Grey?*

A: Probably not, unless you are prepared to deal with all of the trials and tribulations that come with breeding birds. Many people wrongly think that they will make money by breeding birds, assuming that it's as simple at putting two African Greys together and raking in the profits. Nothing could be farther from the truth. The money you will make selling the babies that your birds produce will go into breeding supplies, veterinary visits, food for the babies, and so on. Think carefully before you take on such a large task.

Q: *Why do African Greys always seem to be scratching and picking at themselves?*

A: African Greys, like other birds, are fastidious about their

feathers. They preen all day long to make sure that each feather is clean and in place. If your bird's feathers are shiny and beautiful, all of this "picking" is probably normal preening behavior. If you notice bald patches on your bird, or if your bird's feathers begin to look very shabby, make an appointment with your avian veterinarian.

Q: *How often do African Greys bathe?*

A: How often an African Grey bathes depends on the weather and whether or not you offer him a shallow dish of water to bathe in. If you offer an appealing bath, your African Grey is more likely to bathe. Many African Greys loathe bathing, but this depends on the individual bird.

You should probably not breed your African Grey until you have seriously considered all of the effort, time, money, and care you will have to put into this endeavor.

If you want to house your African Grey with a bird of another species, make sure that both birds are happy with the arrangement. Younger Greys seem more accepting of other species.

Q: *Should I cover my African Grey's cage at night?*

A: If your African Grey is very noisy in the morning or if there's a draft near the bird's cage, you can cover the cage at night for eight to ten hours. Your African Grey might enjoy the darkness and the warmth the cover offers. Make sure that the cover does not develop holes or become threadbare, as this can lead to injury.

Q: *Other than seed, is there some other type of food I should supply? Do I need to buy vitamins?*

A: Your avian veterinarian is the appropriate person to determine the best diet for your African Grey. However, if you feed your bird a very balanced, healthy diet, your bird should not need supplements. Some African Greys will not eat everything you feed them, so a supplement might be in order. Offering foods rich in calcium, such as almonds, dark, leafy greens, tofu, and Brussels sprouts will help to prevent the common problem of calcium deficiency. Strangely enough, spinach does not contribute calcium to the body and can actually decrease absorption, so feed it sparingly.

Q: *I can't seem to find a spot that is draft free. How much of a draft can my African Grey handle?*

A: Most parrots do not like drafts at all. If you can't find a draft-free spot in your home, consider putting up a screen or place a sheet of clear acrylic over the side of the cage where the draft enters it.

Q: *Why does my African Grey flap his wings in his cage? Does that mean he wants to fly even though I have his wings clipped?*

A: Wing-flapping is a typical behavior for clipped African Greys (and flighted African Greys, too). Flapping is like doing birdy jumping jacks, a way of letting out some tension and getting some exercise. This does not necessarily mean that your bird wants to fly, but it doesn't mean that he is not missing the work of flying, either.

Q: *Can I house my African Grey with other birds?*

A: This depends on the individual bird and how the bird was raised, though an African Grey can injure a much smaller bird. If you want to house your African Grey with a bird of another species, you must make sure that both birds are happy with the arrangement. A young African Grey is far more likely to accept a bird of another species than an older African Grey. Don't ever put your birds together just because you want them to get along—it might be dangerous

Q: *How can I positively identify my African Grey if he gets lost or stolen?*

A: There is really no way to positively identify your African Grey once he's in someone else's hands. However, your veterinarian can inject your African Grey with a microchip that contains a traceable number unique to your individual bird. Most avian veterinarians and animal shelters own a scanner. The microchip is about the size of a grain of rice, goes into the breast muscle, and doesn't hurt the bird once he's been injected. The number on the microchip is registered with the company that produces it and proves ownership—if you sell or give away your bird, you can change the ownership records with the company. You can also register your bird's DNA with a

Because free-flying your African Grey is extremely dangerous, a safe solution is to provide him with a large enclosed space in which to fly.

company, but it might be more difficult to get the person who has your Grey to submit to DNA testing than to being scanned for a chip.

Q: *I've heard about people free-flying their African Greys in the open sky. What does this mean and should I do it?*

A: Some people free-fly their large birds in unprotected areas because they believe that even captive birds should fly, though most people choose to keep their Greys clipped. These African Greys are free to mingle with wild birds, land on electric wires, and are easy prey for hawks and other predators. Birds should have the opportunity to fly, but it is a risky endeavor to allow an African Grey to free-fly over a suburban neighborhood.

Some bird theme parks and nature centers may have free-flying African Greys, but people don't often hear about the losses they incur. Also, how can you be certain that your African Grey will return to you once you let him go into the wild blue yonder? A better option is to build a large enclosed space for your African Grey to fly. Most homes have room for a screened patio, which can be wired-over for safety. Homes in cold climates may have space for a sunroom where an African Grey can have some flying time.

APPENDIX: Toxic and Non-Toxic Plants

TOXIC PLANTS

Partial List of Toxic Indoor Plants
Amaryllis (bulbs)
American Yew
Avocado
Azalea (leaves)
Balsam Pear (seeds, outer rind of fruit)
Baneberry (berries, root)
Bird of Paradise (seeds)
Black Locust
Blue-green Algae (some forms toxic)
Boxwood (leaves, stems)
Buckthorn (fruit, bark)
Buttercup (sap, bulbs)
Caladium (leaves)
Calla Lily (leaves)
Castor Bean (also castor oil, leaves)
Chalice Vine/Trumpet Vine
Christmas Candle (sap)
Clematis/Virginia
Coral Plant (seeds)
Cowslip
Daffodil (bulbs)
Daphne (berries)
Datura – berries
Deadly Amanita
Death Camas
Delphinium
Dieffenbachia/Dumb Cane (leaves)
Eggplant (fruit okay)
Elephant's Ear/Taro (leaves, stem)
English Ivy (berries, leaves)
English Yew
False Henbane
Fly Agaric Mushroom
Foxglove (leaves, seeds)

Golden Chain/Laburnum
Hemlock
Henbane (seeds)
Holly (berries)
Horse Chestnut/Buckeye (nuts, twigs)
Hyacinth (bulbs)
Hydrangea (flower bud)
Indian Turnip
Iris/Blue Flag (bulbs)
Jack-in-the-Pulpit
Japanese Yew (needles, seeds)
Java Bean (uncooked)
Juniper (needles, stems, berries)
Lantana (immature berries)
Larkspur
Laurel
Lily of the Valley
Lobelia
Locoweed
Lords and Ladies/Cuckoopint
Marijuana/Hemp (leaves)
Mayapple (fruit is safe)
Mescal Beans (seeds)
Mistletoe (berries)
Mock Orange (fruit)
Monkshood - leaves, root
Morning Glory
Narcissus (bulbs)
Nightshade (all varieties)
Oleander
Philodendron (leaves and stem)
Poinsettia
Poison Ivy (sap)
Poison Oak (sap)
Pokeweed/Inkberry
Potato (eyes, new shoots)
Privet
Rhododendron
Rhubarb (leaves)
Rosary Peas/Indian Licorice

Skunk Cabbage
Snowdrop
Snow on the Mountain
Sweet Pea - seeds, fruit
Tobacco (leaves)
Virginia Creeper (sap)
Water Hemlock
Western Yew
Wisteria
Yam bean

Partial List of Toxic Outdoor Plants

Acacia
Apricot (fruit is safe)
Autumn Crocus/Meadow Saffron
Beans (raw)
Birch
Bittersweet Nightshade
Bleeding Heart/Dutchman's Breeches
Bloodroot
Bracken Fern
Broomcorn Grass
Candelabra Tree
Cardinal Flower
Cherry Tree (bark, twigs, leaves, pits)
Chinaberry Tree
Crown of Thorns
Croton
Elderberry
Euonymus/Spindle Tree
False Hellebore
Ficus (weeping)
Firethorn/Pyracantha
Four O'Clock
Glory Bean
Ground Cherry
Honey Locust
Honeysuckle
Horsetail
Indian Licorice Bean

Ivy
Jasmine
Jimsonweed/Thornapple
Jerusalem Cherry (berries)
Johnson Grass
Kentucky Coffee Tree
Lupines/Bluebonnet
Mandrake
Mango Tree (fruit is safe)
Moonseed
Mountain Laurel
Mushrooms (many kinds)
Nectarine (pit and parts of tree)
Nettles
Nutmeg
Oak (acorns, foliage)
Peach (pit and parts of tree)
Peanuts (raw)
Pencil Tree
Periwinkle
Pigweed
Pikeweed
Pine (needles, berries)
Plum
Pothos
Prune
Rain Tree
Ranunculus/Buttercup
Red Maple
Sandbox Tree
Scarlet Runner Beans
Snowflake
Sorghum Grass
Sorrel
Sudan Grass
Tansy Ragwort
Vetch
Yellow Jasmine
Yew (needles, thistles)
Yucca

Non-Toxic/Safe Plants

Partial List of Non-Toxic/Safe Houseplants
Acacia Aloe
African Violet
Baby's Tears
Bamboo
Begonia
Bougainvillea
Chickweed
Christmas Cactus
Cissus/Kangaroo Vine
Coffee
Coleus
Corn Plant
Crabapple
Dandelion
Dogwood
Donkey Tail
Dracena Varieties
Ferns
Figs
Gardenia
Grape Ivy
Hens and Chickens
Herbs
Jade Plant
Kalanchoe
Marigold
Monkey Plant
Mother-in-Law's Tongue
Nasturtium
Natal Plum
Nettle
Pepperomia
Petunia
Pittosporum
Prayer Plant
Purple Passion/Velvet
Schefflera (Umbrella)

Sensitive Plant
Spider Plant
Swedish Ivy
Thistle
Wandering Jew
White Clover
Zebra Plant

Partial List of Non-Toxic/Safe Outdoor Plants
American Bittersweet
Apple
Arbutus
Ash
Aspen
Autumn Olive
Bamboo
Barberry
Bayberry
Beech
Birch
Bladdernut
Blueberry
Citrus (any)
Coralberry
Cotoneaster
Cottonwood
Crabapple
Dogwood
Elderberry
Elm
Eucalyptus
Fir
Firethorn
Grape Vine
Guava
Hawthorn
Huckleberry
Larch
Madrona

Magnolia
Manzanita
Marigold
Nasturtium
Norfolk Island Pine
Nuts (not chestnut or oak)
Palms
Pear
Pine
Poplar
Pyracantha
Raspberry
Rose
Sequoia (Redwood)
Snowberry
Spruce
Viburnum
Wax Plant
White Poplar
Willow

RESOURCES

ORGANIZATIONS

African Parrot Society
http://www.wingscc.com/aps/

American Federation of Aviculture
P.O. Box 7312
N. Kansas City, MO 64116
Telephone: (816) 421-2473
Fax: (816) 421-3214
E-mail: afaoffice@aol.com
http://www.afa.birds.org/

Avicultural Society of America
P.O. Box 5516
Riverside, CA 92517-5516
Telephone: (909) 780-4102
Fax: (909) 789-9366
E-mail: info@asabirds.org
http://www.asabirds.org/index.php

Aviculture Society of the United Kingdom
Arcadia-The Mounts-East Allington-Totnes
Devon TQ9 7QJ
United Kingdom
E-mail: admin@avisoc.co.uk
http://www.avisoc.co.uk/

World Parrot Trust
US Administrator: Joanna Eckles
WPT-USA P.O. Box 353
Stillwater, MN 55082
Telephone: (651) 275-1877
Fax: (651) 275-1891
E-mail: info@worldparrottrust.org
http://www.worldparrottrust.org/

PUBLICATIONS

Bird Talk Magazine
3 Burroughs
Irvine, CA 92618
Telephone: (949) 855-8822
Fax: (949) 855-3045
http://www.animalnetwork.com/
birdtalk/default.asp

Parrots Magazine
P.O. Box 386
Goleta, CA 93116-0386
Telephone: (800) 294-7951
Fax: (978) 246-0209
http://www.parrotmag.com/

Winged Wisdom Magazine
Birds n Ways
39760 Calle Bellagio
Temecula, CA 92592
Telephone: (909) 303-9376
http://www.birdsnways.com/wisdom/
index.htm#toc

INTERNET RESOURCES

The Complete Lexicon of Parrots
(http://www.arndt-verlag.com/
index.html)
As its name implies, this website contains a wealth of information on virtually every parrot breed imaginable, with detailed notes on diet, breeding, habits, and physical descriptions.

RESOURCES

The Parrot Pages
(http://www.parrotpages.com)
This website includes links to many different bird organizations, online magazines, veterinary organizations, species information, and bird-related upcoming events.

VETERINARY RESOURCES

Association of Avian Veterinarians (AAV)
P.O. Box 811720
Boca Raton, FL 33481-1720
Telephone: (561) 393-8901
Fax: (561) 393-8902
E-mail: AAVCTRLOFC@aol.com
http://www.aav.org/

EMERGENCY RESOURCES AND RESCUE ORGANIZATIONS

ASPCA Animal Poison Control Center
Telephone: (888) 426-4435
E-mail: napcc@aspca.org (for non-emergency, general information only)
http://www.apcc.aspca.org

Bird Hotline
P.O. Box 1411
Sedona, AZ 86339-1411
E-mail: birdhotline@birdhotline.com
http://www.birdhotline.com/

Feathered Friends Adoption and Rescue
222 S.W. Dillon Ct.
Port St. Lucie, FL 34953-6203
Telephone: (772) 343-8935
Fax: (772) 344-7237
E-mail: jesbirds@msn.com
http://hometown.aol.com/MAHorton/FFAP.html

INDEX

PHOTO CREDITS: